The Life of the Spirit
in the World of Today

The Life of the Spirit
in the World of Today

GORDON S. WAKEFIELD

Epworth Press

Acknowledgment is made to Faber & Faber for permission
to reprint from "Little Gidding" from T. S. Eliot's *Four Quartets*
and to John Murray Ltd. and John Betjeman for permission to
reprint from *In a Bath Tea-Shop* from John Betjeman's *Collected
Poems*.

FIRST PUBLISHED BY
The Macmillan Company
in the United States of America
PUBLISHED IN GREAT BRITAIN BY
Epworth Press 1970
(Book Steward
Frank H. Cumbers)
SBN 7162 0111 9

For
B E R Y L
with all my love

Contents

Introduction

"Spirituality" is one of the fashionable words of our time in religious circles, yet, like so many useful and comprehensive terms, it is not easy to define. It originated with M. l'Abbé Pourrat, who distinguished between dogmatic theology, which deals with the content of Christian faith, moral theology, which is concerned with the principles of Christian conduct and spiritual theology, which is most important of all, because its subject matter is Christian life itself. Dom Robert Petitpierre, of the Anglican Benedictines of Nashdom Abbey, Buckinghamshire, England, has suggested that a good rendering of the French *spiritualité* might be "The Art of Christian Living."

The spirit is the life of man, that which makes him different from a cabbage or one of the other animals. To admit this is not to tie ourselves to any untenable dualism of body and spirit, or to the anthropology of the Genesis story about God breathing into man's nostrils the breath of life, though this is a good mythological expression of what man uniquely has—animation, "spiritedness," powers of thought and speech.

Christianity has always claimed that the spirit of man can live and grow only by union with God in Christ. This union is supremely sustained and expressed in prayer and worship, though it does, of course, affect everything a man does, the whole of his behavior, all his attitudes.

Today this is being questioned. The age in which we live is not congenial to the old practices of spirituality, but the real uncertainty concerns the presuppositions of the Christian faith itself. What do we mean by God? Is prayer more than a soliloquy, which the universe may echo but cannot answer? Is the Christian world view any longer tenable for honest men who are facing the realities of our time?

My own interest in spirituality springs from the pastoral work and conduct of worship of a Methodist minister. More academically it has been represented by studies of *Puritan Devotion* (1957) and *Methodist Devotion* (1966), both published by the Epworth Press, London, of which I have been editor since 1963. In 1965, I became joint study-secretary with Father Mark Gibbard, S.S.J.E., of a working party set up by the British Council of Churches "to consider how the spirituality of the member churches might be studied with a view to preparing proposals for promoting the spiritual life." It fell to me to write the Report (London: The Epworth Press, 1968). Knowing this, Mr. Clement Alexandre of the Macmillan Company suggested that I use the opportunity also to work on a bigger book on the theme.

What follows is under some obligation to the British Council of Churches group and uses, here and there, by permission of the Epworth Press, some phrases and paragraphs that are found in the Report. But it has been written *de novo* and is a far more general work, related to the American scene. It covers much ground which was not surveyed by the working party and its conclusions are my own. In preparing the typescript, I have taken counsel with no man.

This does not mean that I am not bearing a weight of unpayable debt, which extends, like the chain around Marley's ghost, back across all the years of my adult life. As I wrote, I found myself more and more convinced that a Christian philosophy for our present needs may well be found in the work of Alfred North Whitehead. This brought back to my mind the help I received in my first introduction to Whitehead during World War II, when I read philosophy (without notable success) at Manchester University, England, under the late Professor A. D. Ritchie and Miss (afterwards Professor) Dorothy M. Emmet. It is more than twenty years since I last saw either of them, but gratitude increases.

The person to whom I owe most is my wife, who, though no professional, has typed nearly every folio, and, with cheerful resignation, has watched the weeds sprout in the garden and the household chores be postponed, as every spare minute has been gobbled up by the insatiable literary maw.

GORDON S. WAKEFIELD

Harpenden,
Hertfordshire,
England
Easter 1968

PART I

The Christian Inheritance
of Spiritual Life

1 According to the New Testament

An early name for Christianity was simply *the Way* and perhaps this is the best description from which to begin an account of its long and winding course through the centuries. Christianity was a way of life, *the* Way, its first apostles would have claimed.

In one of the upper room discourses of St. John's Gospel, Jesus says "I am the Way" and none of its exponents, from the first days until now, would dispute the contention that Christianity is Christ, though some might prefer the more sophisticated "the Christ event." Jesus and what happened to him—his life, death and resurrection, the giving of the Holy Spirit to be his representative—determine the direction of Christian living. The Way is his way through the cross to the victory of love. It is an upward path to the perfection of God, which is beyond this world and it involves every part of a man, every moment; it cannot be traveled without a crucifixion of self, which is not a once-for-all dramatic paroxysm but a daily dying. "If any man will come after me, let him deny himself and take up his cross daily and follow me."

The Way is not traveled alone. Just as Bunyan's *Pilgrim's Progress* is no solitary affair, but is undertaken, in both parts of the book, in company, so from New Testament times, Christians have lived in the com-

3

munity of the Church. It is arguable whether apart from the Church and its corporate memory there would be a Christ at all.[1] It is certain that more than any other religion, Judaism possibly excepted, Christianity depends on the fellowship of believers and their meeting together for worship, prayer and the sharing of experience, all of which recall Christ and the gospel. "They devoted themselves to the apostles' teaching and fellowship, to the breaking of bread and the prayers." (Acts 2:42) "Let us consider how to stir up one another to love and good works, not neglecting to meet together, as is the habit of some, but encouraging one another, and all the more as you see the day drawing near." (Hebrews 10:24–25)

Much of Christian worship and prayer has been derived from the spirituality of the Jews. In New Testament times this stood in great contrast to the mixture of skepticism and superstition with which the Hellenistic world regarded religious exercises. From the synagogue, the early Christians took over the "ministry of the word"—the reading and exposition of scripture in a setting of praise and prayer, in which the Psalms figured prominently. Like the Jews, they kept a special holy day each week, though they transferred it from the seventh day to the first to commemorate Christ's resurrection and to emphasize their distinctness, although Christian sabbatarianism was not possible in ancient Rome. They also observed the "hours" of prayer. The Jews recited the Shema (Deut. 6:4–9; 11:13–21; Num. 15:41) in the morning and evening

[1] Cf. John Knox, *The Church and the Reality of Christ*, New York, 1962.

and in addition prayed the eighteen benedictions in the morning and at the times of the afternoon and evening sacrifices. The Acts of the Apostles describes Peter and John going to the temple for the afternoon prayers (Acts 3:1), while the *Didache*, which more scholars are now dating as an early work, lays down that the Lord's Prayer is to be used three times a day.[2] The Christians practiced fasting too, although there was a tradition that Jesus and his immediate circle had not fasted (Mark 2:18–22) and an insistence in some quarters that Christian fasting was a discipline of the new age which Jesus had inaugurated, very different from the old dispensation.

Christians in fact supplemented, modified and transformed the liturgical customs of the Jews. Their prayer broke through the ancient formalities and could not be confined to the regular hours. They composed their own prayers, hymns and spontaneous "spiritual songs." They repeated a prayer which Jesus himself had taught them, which addressed God in terms of great intimacy as Father, "Abba, Father," and was dominated by the thought of the coming kingdom. They used certain rites which they believed Jesus himself had instituted. The Christian Church was entered by the sacrament of Baptism, a dipping in water which was a dramatic and, it was believed, effective sign of death to the old life and resurrection to the new. But the staple act of Christian worship was the eucharistic meal. The origins of this are obscure but it would seem reasonable to discern a connection between the meals which Jesus had with his followers both before and after the

[2] See J. Jeremias, *The Prayers of Jesus*, London, 1967, p. 66 ff.

resurrection, as recorded in all of the four gospels, and "the breaking of bread" which is singled out as a liturgical custom in the Acts of the Apostles. (e.g., Acts 2:42; 20:7) This breaking of bread was a ceremonial act which took place when Christians met in each other's private homes on the first day of the week to eat together, to pray and talk, or, probably more often, to listen to preaching and teaching.

Paul regards the custom as one of extreme solemnity and relates it, according to apostolic tradition, to an act of Jesus on his betrayal night, by which he invested his anticipated death with atoning power, which would be conveyed to his followers through sacramental channels.

For I received from the Lord what I also delivered to you, that the Lord Jesus on the night when he was betrayed took bread, and when he had given thanks, he broke it, and said "This is my body which is for you. Do this in remembrance of me." In the same way also the cup, after supper, saying, "This cup is the new covenant in my blood. Do this, as often as you drink it, in remembrance of me." For as often as you eat this bread and drink this cup, you proclaim the Lord's death until he comes. (1 Cor. 11:23–26)

John also, though he tells of no institution or command of Christ, writes in the most vivid terms of Jesus as the Bread of Life, whose bread is his flesh given for the life of the world.

Truly, truly, I say to you, unless you eat the flesh of the Son of man and drink his blood, you have no life in you; he who eats my flesh and drinks my blood has eternal life, and I will raise him up at the last day. For my flesh is food indeed, and my blood is drink indeed. He who eats my flesh and drinks my blood abides in me, and I in him. As the living Father sent me, and I live because of the Father, so he who eats me will live because of me. This is the bread which came down from heaven, not such as the fathers ate and died; he who eats this bread will live forever. (John 6:53–58)

From these fertile seeds did the eucharistic theology and sacramental devotion of the Christian ages spring up and flourish.

DEVELOPMENTS WITHIN THE NEW TESTAMENT: HISTORY AND ESCHATOLOGY

Those who joined the Christian Way did so at many different points, via many different routes and were people of diverse temperaments and styles.

For all there was in some sense the attraction of Christ, mediated by the story the Church told and the life of the Christian community itself. The Church early began to relate the Christ event to the previous history of the Jews and the sculptured sarcophagi of the catacombs support the inference that "another important factor in Christianity's success in the Roman Empire was its possession of a sacred literature which comprised an abundance of vivid narrative about events of great dramatic appeal." [3]

The common background of all types of Christian experience in New Testament times was the belief that

[3] S. G. F. Brandon, *The Modern Churchman*, VI, no. 1, October 1962, 29–30.

the kingdom of God was at hand and that the affairs of this world were soon to be wound up. This gave a note of crisis to Christian prayer "Our Lord come!", "Amen. Come, Lord Jesus!"

"Lead us not into temptation" or "Do not bring us to the test in the death throes of this age."

"Stay awake, all of you; and pray that you may be spared the test."

"Pray that it may not come in winter."

"Will not God vindicate his chosen, who cry out to him day and night, while he listens patiently to them?"

"I tell you he will vindicate them soon enough."

In the course of the New Testament, we see this primitive eschatology modified. In the fourth gospel, for instance, there is still the promise of Christ's coming, but there is no apocalyptic, no lurid and hectic warning of the collapse of the outward order. Christ will come with the Father to believers and there will be mutual indwelling. (John 14:23)

OBSERVERS OF THE LAW

Many of the writings of the New Testament and of the early Church imply communities of Christians for whom the following of the Way was 99 percent obedience. These inspired the Letter of James, the Gospel of Matthew and the *Didache* with its choice of the two ways—life or death. They lived by the new law of the gospel, which was increasingly interpreted not by private judgment but by the magisterium of the Church. They sought to keep the commandments as reinterpreted by Christ and had to be reminded that true religion meant good works, that Christ often came in the disguise of the needy, and that the law itself might be a barrier to perfection if one's aims were confined to the letter rather than to the spirit. For them prayer would be regular and liturgical, though usually with words going beyond set forms rather like nineteenth-century Methodists at a prayer meeting.

It is significant that there are two accounts of the giving of the Lord's Prayer in the gospels. The one in Luke (11:1 ff.), a gospel written for gentiles, sees the prayer as an encouragement to Christians to persist in asking. They must be as importunate as a man caught unawares who desperately needs bread. The original context may have been the crisis of the coming kingdom. Christians are to approach God—dread judge of all as he is—as their Father to ask for a speedy inauguration of his reign on earth, deliverance from the worst trials and disasters, and the privilege of eating bread with him in his kingdom. Luke does not feel that matters are quite so urgent as this and recoils from a naked petition for the satisfying of material needs and so suggests that what Christians should ask for so vehemently is the Holy Spirit. But prayer is asking and ordinary Church members (converts from paganism) without any particular religious background or spiritual experience must learn simply to pour out their requests to God as children to a Father with whom they are on intimate terms.

In Matthew (6:9 ff.), the gospel for Jewish Christians, the prayer is given to those who may well have been taught methods of devotion from childhood, methods whose danger is legalistic formality or ostentatious babbling. They must practice an economy of words, a series of brief petitions uttered in faith that God, their Father, knows their necessities before they ask and does not need to be told them with great elaboration of detail or honorific compliments. They must pray quietly and in secret, meditatively rather than verbosely, and without telling the world how devout they are. Here again the teaching is for simple believers, though they may be conventionally religious. As Christians they will continue to live by rule though it will be less elaborate, less conspicuous, less burdensome and inspired by an altogether freer, closer and more personal relationship to God than in Judaism. But prayer must be regular and, just as in the case of those for whom Luke was written, it must be incessant. At the same time no rule of life is specifically prescribed in the New Testament. For many of the poor and enslaved it would have been a preposterous irrelevancy.

PENTECOSTALISTS

Other Christians were Pentecostalists, claiming an immediate inspiration which manifested itself in the phenomena of "enthusiasm," such as speaking with tongues and superrational excitement. The early Christians heard voices, saw visions, went into trances and received what they recognized as divine guidance by sortilege and dreams. They could be inspired to ecstatic frenzy, which must at times have resembled the uninhibited stamping and screaming of young people today in the presence of a pop star. They needed

apostolic restraint from exhibitionism, intolerance, im-
morality and blasphemy. Paul had to show them that
Christ-like love was the token of the Spirit's possession,
the only sign that they were partakers of the divine
nature. Pentecostalists were apt to make light of form
and order; to pray only when they were under the
direct influence of the Spirit, and to regard every utterance while they were in a "spiritual state" as inspired,
whether it was intelligible or edifying or not. These
were, however, the extremists, notoriously at Corinth.
The Pentecostalists of Acts are so possessed that spec-
tators regard them as drunk or mad. They sometimes
take, under the Spirit's guidance, such decisions as in
a more composed hour would be branded as irrespon-
sible, but their enthusiasm is contained by the rites
and disciplines of the new community. "They continued steadfastly in the apostles' teaching and fellowship, in the breaking of bread and the prayers." (Acts
2:42)

The great theologians of the New Testament—Paul
and John—teach a true Pentecostalism. The gift of the
Holy Spirit is the *sine qua non* of the Christian life.
It is because of the gift of the Spirit that we can say
the Lord's Prayer.

"To prove that you are sons, God has sent into our
hearts the Spirit of his son, crying 'Abba! Father!'"
(Gal. 4:6)

"For all who are moved by the Spirit of God are sons
of God. The Spirit you have received is not a spirit of
slavery leading you back into a life of fear, but a Spirit
that makes us sons, enabling us to cry 'Abba! Father!'"
(Rom. 8:14–15)

"In the same way the Spirit comes to the aid of our weakness. We do not even know how we ought to pray, but through our inarticulate groans the Spirit himself is pleading for us." (Rom. 8:26)

The last is a passage of most profound importance, which has received the close attention of Tillich and Gregor Smith in our own day.[4] It certainly points to a prayer which transcends formalism and words, a prayer which recognizes our helplessness in the world before God and the inadequacy of all rules and methods; these may be an insult to a crucified world and a crucified God alike, as well as to the majesty and wonder of the universe. Open to the Spirit and dependent on him alone we may so pray as to cooperate with God in his purpose of love.

THE CAPTIVE OF GRACE

But this is Paul, an apostle of towering spiritual genius and perceptions. He belongs to our third category, as does Augustine centuries later. These Christians are few in number but of tremendous importance. They believed that they were on the Way through no decision of their own unaided wills but because God had arrested them in their former tracks and turned them round and placed them there. Paul believed himself called of God, made Christ's by divine initiative and in spite of himself. He gave much moral instruc-

---

[4] See, e.g., the sermons in Paul Tillich, *The Shaking of the Foundations*, New York, 1948 and *The New Being*, New York, 1956, and R. Gregor Smith, *Secular Christianity*, London, 1966, p. 205 ff.

tion and preached the law of Christ, but this was the
consequence not the cause of "grace"—God's love in
action to rescue him. He was violently opposed to
Jewish legalism and in this was probably like Jesus,
who set himself against the religious system of his day
in the name of divine compassion.

This type of religious experience has had incalculable
effect on Christian theology. Many regard it as alone
giving the clue to the authentic gospel, both the gospel
Jesus preached and the gospel about Jesus. I myself
stand, intellectually, on this side of the evangelical-
catholic frontier. But it is doubtful if the majority of
Christians adherents do, or ever have, and there are
certainly other strains in the New Testament, as we
have tried to show. Kenneth Kirk declared that, had
Paul lived half a century or a century later, his indig-
nant wonder evoked by the legalism of the Galatians
would have increased a hundred-fold. "The example
of the Galatians might be thought to have infected the
whole Christian Church; writer after writer seems to
have little other interest than to express the genius of
Christianity wholly in terms of law and obedience,
reward and punishment." [5]

In Paul's own prayers, thanksgiving is dominant. "An
expression of thanksgiving occurs immediately after the
greeting in every extant Pauline Epistle except Galatians and (if they be Pauline) I Timothy and Titus." [6]
In the great prayer of the first chapter of Colossians a
thanksgiving for light, for love and for rescue from evil,

[5] Kenneth E. Kirk, *The Vision of God*, London, 1932, p. 111.
[6] C. F. D. Moule, *Colossians and Philemon*, The Cambridge
Greek Testament Commentary, Cambridge, 1957, p. 47.

follows a petition for sensitiveness to God's will, Christian conduct and strength. But this springs from an antecedent thanksgiving based on God's deed in Christ. "The solid fact of what God has done is always the 'perch' (so to speak) from which Christian prayer takes its flight and to which it returns." [7] This is only to be expected in the light of Paul's own experience.

Paul clearly prayed much for other people, both in his own churches and in those founded by others, like Rome and Colossae.

> We give thanks to God always for you all, constantly mentioning you in our prayers. (Thess. 1:2)
> For God is my witness, whom I serve with my spirit in the gospel of his Son, that without ceasing I mention you always in my prayers. (Romans 1:9)
> I thank my God in all my remembrances of you, always in every prayer of mine for you all making my prayer with joy. (Phil. 1:3–4)

The comparatively late I Timothy exhorts that "supplications, prayers, intercessions, thanksgivings be made for all men." (2:1) There is a saying of Jesus: "Pray for them that persecute you." (Matt. 6:44; Luke 6:28) Presumably this is to be a prayer for their forgiveness such as some manuscripts record of Jesus on the Cross (Luke 23:34) and is also attributed to the first Christian martyr, Stephen. (Acts 7:60) But much Christian prayer was, as it has continued to be, confined to the household of faith. No New Testament writer specifically questions the appropriateness of prayer for all mankind since presumably they all had a simple faith in God who knew the way to men's

[7] *Ibid.*, p. 48.

hearts and whose power was at work to convert the unthinking, ignorant and sinful. Neither did Paul's doctrine of election, the reluctant consequence of his attempt to reconcile his fellow Jews' large-scale rejection of the gospel with the mercy and omnipotence of God, lead him to assert, as did some of the extreme Puritans in the seventeenth century, that we ought not to pray for those whom God may not intend to save. The Church of the second century regarded intercession, as it did the saying of the Lord's Prayer and the celebration of the Eucharist, as an activity of the baptized alone, after the catechumens had departed;[8] it included prayers for all men. But throughout the centuries Christian intercession has not always been as comprehensive as the injunctions of Jesus and I Timothy would seem to demand. It has sometimes been almost spiteful against "Jews, Turks, infidels and heretics," prayer in a vituperative tone, with harsh enmity ill-concealed, humble before God, haughty toward men.

The sophisticated demurrer that it may not be Christianly possible to pray for *all* men or to love all in a way commensurate with the cost of loving, has had to wait until our own time. In one of the pregnant and most memorable passages of *I and Thou*, Martin Buber wrote:

Love is the responsibility of an *I* for a *Thou*. In this lies the likeness—impossible in any feeling whatsoever— of all who love, from the smallest to the greatest and

[8] This is stated in *The Apostolic Tradition of Hippolytus*. See edition of Gregory Dix, London, 1937 and 1968, p. 39; and implied in Justin's *Apology*, I, 65.

from the blessedly protected man, whose life is rounded in that of a loved being, to him who is all his life nailed to the cross of the world, and who ventures to bring himself to the dreadful point—to love *all men*.[9]

Intercessory prayer might be defined in the same terms, but as a development of the hints and precepts of the Hebrew and Christian scriptures, not by simple exegesis.

Paul speaks of "the mystery" (Ephesians and Colossians), a secret or hidden knowledge of God revealed to Christians. But this does not require any elaborate spiritual technique; it is the divine purpose itself which, though it may be hidden from the worldly-wise, is available to the humblest believer. It is God's free gift, though clearly it is not to be regarded lightly and the acceptance of it takes all that a man has.

Paul uses the phrase "in Christ" more than 150 times. Yet this is not a state reached by prayer but by faith. It must be understood corporately. To be "in Christ" is no "flight of the alone to the alone"; it is to be in the body of Christ, the fellowship of believers, the Church. Like John, Paul speaks of mutual indwelling. We are in Christ and he is in us. But this is no absorption into the infinite. The relationship is personal and the union is with Christ in his dying and rising again, his fulfillment of the purpose of God, or, as C. H. Dodd put it, members of the Church are "placed ever anew within the eschatological crisis in which it had its origin." [10]

"I have been crucified with Christ," says Paul, "yet

[9] Martin Buber, *I and Thou*, translated by Ronald Gregor Smith, Edinburgh, 1937.
[10] C. H. Dodd, *History and the Gospel*, London, 1938, p. 163.

I live; and yet no longer I, but Christ liveth in me; and that life which I now live in the flesh I live in faith, the faith which is in the Son of God, who loved me and gave himself for me." (Gal. 2:20)

PROPHETIC OR MYSTICAL PRAYER?

In the New Testament, prayer—and this goes for all three of the types of experience we distinguish—is, to use Heiler's famous distinction, much more prophetic than mystical. "Mystical prayer has its roots in the yearning of the devout person for union with the infinite; prophetic prayer arises from the profound need of the heart and the longing for salvation and grace. Mystical prayer is artificially prepared through a refined psychological technique of meditation; the prophetic petition breaks forth spontaneously and violently from the subconscious depths of the religious soul that has been deeply stirred. Mystical prayer is silent contemplative delight; prophetic prayer a passionate crying and groaning, vehement complaining and pleading. Mystical prayer is solemn exaltation of the spirit to the highest good; prophetic prayer is simple outpouring of the heart. Mystical prayer is a passing out of oneself, an entering and sinking into the infinite God; prophetic prayer is the utterance of the profound need that moves the inmost being.

Mystical prayer is a weary climbing by degrees to the heights of vision and union with God; prophetic prayer a stormy assault upon the Father's heart." [11]

Heiler's dichotomy is too sharp, his definition of

[11] F. Heiler, *Prayer*, New York, 1958, p. 283–84.

mysticism too arbitrary and generalized. The word covers too many varieties of spirituality in world religions to be susceptible of such sweeping terms, which certainly do not do justice to many Christian mystics. But when Heiler writes of prophetic or faith piety he is describing the religion of the Bible, and of the New Testament as well as the Old. The question is whether this is in fact incompatible with a certain type of mysticism. It has been suggested that much mystical experience approximates what Lindblöm has called the "concentration ecstasy" of the Hebrew prophets and that there are parallels between the Lady Julian of Norwich, fourteenth-century English mystic, and Jeremiah, most prophetic of the prophets in Heiler's sense.[12] We may agree that the roots of later mysticism are in Paul's and John's language of union with Christ and in the Eucharist, which latter, simple as its actions and elements are, has limitless riches of symbol and imagery. Since Heiler first wrote, scholarship has become more sensitive both to the liturgical background of the New Testament and to the mystical element in liturgy itself, the inner meaning of the outward rite and the power which the symbols have to carry the worshiper beyond the things of time and sense into unity with the eternal.

THE NATURE AND THE DESTINY OF MAN

It remains to notice that the spirituality of the New Testament presupposes the continuation of the Chris-

[12] See E. J. Tinsley, "The Bible and Mysticism," *The York Quarterly*, November 1957, p. 10 ff.

tian life after death. The real death of the believer is
what baptism symbolizes, his sharing in the death and
resurrection of the Lord Jesus; after this, his mortal
passage is but an incident. But the immortality of the
soul is not, as it has been fashionable to say in recent
years, an altogether Greek concept, alien to the Christian gospel, which proclaims only the stupendous miracle of resurrection, the restoration by God of what we
should call the whole personality, with the renewed
human race, at the last day. This modern emphasis on
resurrection, rather than on immortality, is congenial
to the natural skepticism so prevalent in our time—the
Protestant continental theologians' insistence that we
have neither knowledge nor anthropological hope, only
faith in a God who brings life out of absolute death,
and to the secular Christian whose gospel is that we
have only this life and that other worldliness is the
great distraction. It fits the facts of brute experience
—the ambiguities of spiritualism and psychic research
apart—and makes for powerful if puzzling and perhaps
distressing sermons. But it is not what the New Testament teaches.

True, Paul is not consistent. But he wrote 2 Corinthians 5 as well as 1 Corinthians 15. Admittedly the
latter passage is less confused in its metaphors, more
confident in its assertion that, although, after death,
Christians will sleep in bodiless nakedness, there will
be at the end a glorious resurrection when "death is
swallowed up in victory." But in 2 Corinthians Paul
affirms that after death we are not naked in Sheol but
clothed with what he calls a house and a tent, which

also serves as a garment. To be absent from the body is to be at home with the Lord.

Similarly, in Philippians, to live in this world is Christ, and yet to die is gain, for this means to depart and be with him. John, too, implies that Jesus is the Way, who leads through this world to the place prepared for his followers with him and the Father. It is legitimate, therefore, to say with C. K. Barrett: "Man as man is not immortal; neither as man is he assured of resurrection. As Christian, as the new man, he receives a present life that assures him of future life, and a preliminary resurrection that assures him of final resurrection; may we not say that he receives a kind of immortality in the assurance that God will raise him up at the last day? Man may be said to become immortal not in his own right as being or having a soul, but because God assures him that he will raise him up at the last day. It is this pregnant compound of gift and promise, that gnostics and orthodox, from the second century onwards, were to rend in two." [13]

What this means for the life of worship and prayer on earth is hinted rather than expounded in the New Testament. Certainly commemoration of the faithful departed belongs to the true worship of him who is "the God of Abraham and Isaac and Jacob"; and Christians probably conceived of the praises of the Church on earth, as of the whole of Christian activity, as being carried on in the sight of the great cloud of witnesses and faintly echoing the perfect worship of

[13] C. K. Barrett, "Immortality and Resurrection," 1964 Drew Lecture on Immortality, New College, London, *London Quarterly* and *Holborn Review*, April 1965, p. 101.

heaven. The Apocalypse implies this. Whether this allows prayer for the departed is less clear—Paul's reference to those who were baptized for the dead is hardly a sufficient foundation. Any thought of a long journey through purgatory on which our prayers may help the souls of the dead would seem alien to scripture and could be destructive of the joy in Christ and in the communion of saints of which scripture is redolent. But it is artificial to distinguish between the inescapable thought of those who have left this world, whatever their conscious relation to Christ, and prayer for them. Meanwhile, according to the New Testament, the life of prayer in the Church on earth is part of that progress along the Way, which leads to the life of the world to come.

2 The Continuing Centuries

The story we have to tell is of the effects of the un-expected continuance of the "present age," both upon the Church's styles of life and upon its reflections on the memory of the Christ event. The early Christians did not see themselves as the progenitors of a vast and complex movement which would influence lands and civilizations they never knew in ages yet unborn. If Paul looked to Spain and Thomas went to India and, much more dubiously, Joseph of Arimathea to Glaston-bury, no apostolic visionary contemplated the Americas!

The story could be written in terms of topography. How much of Christian spirituality is comprehended in "the desert"! There is the perennial influence on Christianity of the wilderness wanderings of old Israel, which have been seen as the type of the Church's existence in East and West alike; the tradition that Jesus was tempted in the desert of Jordan and that Paul went to Arabia; the rise of monasticism in the deserts of Egypt; the belief of mystics, combatted by John Wesley, that a "wilderness state" is inevitable if the soul is to advance toward perfection, the counsel of innumerable spiritual guides that for Christians living in the world there must be a rhythm of advance and withdrawal, involvement and detachment.

"The city" too is an image which figures large in

Christian liturgy and thought, and has its basis firmly in human experience, from the Psalms of David to Augustine's *De Civitate Dei*, from Jesus weeping over the old Jerusalem to the seer's vision of the new Jerusalem coming down out of heaven from God, from Paul's declaration of our heavenly citizenship (with its implications for our mission in the world) to Danté and Charles Williams, and, very differently, Harvey Cox.

"The frontier" is less scriptural but heavily charged with meaning whether we think of the Christians who took their gospel to the bounds of civilization when the Roman Empire collapsed, or those, not always the most orthodox or fully "catholic," who, like the sixth-century Nestorians, and the conservative evangelicals (and of course the Jesuits) endured unspeakable hardships to confront alien peoples at the ends of the earth; or of the frontier in nineteenth-century American life where Methodist camp meetings stirred hearts to whom mitre and crozier would have been antiquarian toys had they had chance to see them, and liturgies would have been meaningless; or of the frontier as a favorite concept of Paul Tillich and of those Christian thinkers in our time like Teilhard de Chardin or Frank Lake, the "clinical theologian" who wish to correlate many varied intellectual disciplines in the quest for reality.

The relation between spirituality and climate is worth an academic thesis. A group of Anglo–Catholics commemorated the centenary of the Oxford Movement in 1933 with a symposium on Northern Catholicism. The co-editor, Dr. N. P. Williams, aided by Tacitus, contrasts the spirituality of Northern peoples, which "is of a mystical and soaring quality, appropriate to dwellers amidst the less genial aspects of nature and beneath 'grey and weeping skies' " with "the realistic temper of the Southern races, which delights in shrines, holy places, relics, images, medals, scapulars, and all the apparatus of pre-Christian folk religion which, it is impossible to doubt, the Church of the fourth and fifth centuries failed to abolish completely and therefore Christianized so far as it could." [1] The religion of New England is certainly different from that of the deep South—Puritanical—reasoned, cultured, restrained, as against passionate, noisy, intellectually narrow and, at times, plaintive. But history is as important as geography here. And why do all Americans seem to a Britisher more American than Roman Catholic, Methodist, Episcopalian, Baptist, Mormon or whatever?

In some ways spirituality is the history of Christianity, for the Church from the first has been a worshiping community not a consortium of philosophers or even theologians. The Church of the fourth century could not admit that Christ was less than God, because it worshiped him. Arius, said Athanasius, has no right to worship a creature; but the Church cannot exist without the worship of Christ.[2] The name of the Greek and Russian Church—Holy Orthodox—means not so much "right doctrine" as "right worship." George Tyrrell (1861-1909), the English Jesuit who incurred so much displeasure from his co-religionists because of his "modernism," was essentially a devotional writer, who maintained that the law of faith was

---

[1] *Northern Catholicism*, London, 1933, pp. xi–xii.
[2] J. Burnaby, *The Belief of Christendom*, London, 1959, p. 75.

the law of prayer, that dogmas should be assessed by their "prayer-value." Clearly there is danger here, the danger that could lead to the justification of the cruel caricature of the Catholic modernist position in the words "There is no God and the Virgin Mary is his mother." If belief in the loveliness and compassion of the Blessed Virgin helps us to pray, never mind the historical truth of the matter or the comparative silence of the New Testament—let us gladly recognize the symbolic value of all the development of the dogmas about her, whereas, since God is mysterious and hard to conceive, we may ignore him or even disbelieve. Another Jesuit, Karl Rahner, has spoken wisely when he deplores theology being dictated by pastoral necessity. Yet, as a matter of fact, Christians have never been able to approach the subject matter of their faith with cold and cerebral impartiality. What has won converts has not been argument but devotion. The secret of Wesley, neat and cultured little Oxford don with not a hair out of place, moving rough colliers to tears and transformation of life, was a mystique of spiritual power. Similarly the Oxford Movement, the Anglo–Catholic revival, in the nineteenth-century Church of England gained its hold, not because of the accuracy of its scholarship or its recovery of the true past of the Church, but because of its sense of the numinous. This was the attraction of Newman and, surprisingly, of Pusey in his sermons. This creates difficulties with peoples of other faiths and those who cannot respond to devotional intensity, though it is inescapable when a way of life rather than an intellectual system is at stake and when the way of life is so much commitment to a Person.

At the same time, we must notice some of the important distinctions in the Christian spirituality of the centuries as we tried to do in the New Testament itself.

GOD-CENTERED AND CHRIST-CENTERED DEVOTION

Eastern Orthodox spirituality would agree that the law of faith is the law of prayer. It would remonstrate strongly with Bishop Robinson's assertion in *Honest to God* that "the intellectual search will condition everything." [3] The way to God is *apophatic* (apophasis = denial). It is by the denial of our customary processes of knowledge and of thought that we may come to know him who can be discovered not by reason but by vision, not by thought but by contemplation. This is not to dethrone the mind. Theophan the Recluse (1815–94) describes prayer as "standing before God with the mind in the heart." [4] It is an act of the whole self but the intellect alone will lead to a religion which is ineffective blasphemy. God is wholly other and our minds unaided are inadequate even to frame the hypothesis of his existence. Indeed to use him as an hypothesis, a means of explaining phenomena, is a profane exploitation of him who is the ground of all being.

[3] *Honest to God*, London, 1963, p. 133. See Vladimir Rodzianko, "Honest to God under the Fathers' Judgement," *Theology*, February 1964.

[4] See *The Art of Prayer*, an Orthodox Anthology, London, 1966.

This spirituality is God-centered. Christ is the Way to the Father and the Jesus Prayer, the repetition of the words "Lord Jesus Christ, Son of God, have mercy upon me," is not to call before our minds the man of Galilee but the incarnate Lord who unites us with God. The great Augustine was a representative of this type. It was Christ alone who was his solace, and no rare, direct contemplation of God which so soon left him in recoil; yet not Christ "known after the flesh," but the Christ of faith who leads men to God. In certain manifestations of Western Christianity, however, it is otherwise.

The Abbot Herwegen of Maria Laach published in 1931 a study of *Christian Art and Mystery*[5] He traces the decline of medieval religious painting in Europe through its treatment of the theme of the last supper. Byzantine art is stiff and stilted, in no sense "personalist," but it does manage to convey the sacramental mystery, the numinous, the divine. Giotto somewhat obscures the sacramental theme; the supper is the last reunion of Jesus and his disciples, essentially a human occasion. Leonardo da Vinci, whose fresco is best known of all, gives a psychological treatment. It is a human drama and Christ is merely the central figure. The eye wanders to speculate on the identity of the apostles. The emphasis is not on "This is my body" but "Lord is it I?" In front of Judas, the saltcellar is seen to have been overturned and the salt spilled upon the

---

[5] I am indebted for this reference and the whole paragraph to an essay by Charles Smyth in *The Church in the World* which concludes A. G. Hebert, ed., *The Parish Communion*, London, 1937.

table. It is Jesus in his human relationships who matters, not the Christ who brings us to God.

Certain schools of modern theology might be disposed to welcome this, though they would deplore its incipient sentimentality as they would that of much post-Renaissance painting, particularly of the suffering Saviour. But in some ways it is the precursor of the "liberal Jesus" theology in which Christianity can be defined as "the acceptance of the gift of the friendship of Jesus." [6]

It is doubtful if this is the New Testament understanding, though it might be argued that it is legitimate twentieth-century development from some hints and passages, and helpful to certain types of men and women today. The early Christians do at times address Jesus directly in prayer, notably the dying Stephen, who commends himself to the Lord, while Paul's anxiety over the "thorn in the flesh" is made the subject of repeated conversations with Christ. (2 Cor. 12) In the earliest Fathers there are private prayers and hymns of praise to Jesus. But Jesus does not continue to appear to his disciples as he did on the walk to Emmaus (though even then he came as a stranger and vanished the moment he was recognized) and Paul insists that Christians no longer know Christ "according to the flesh," that is in a human relationship as the first apostles did in Galilee. The burden of the Johannine teaching has been conveyed in some profound words of the Cambridge scholar F. J. A. Hort, who wrote of "the transition from a presence taking its

[6] Leslie D. Weatherhead, *The Transforming Friendship*, London, 1928, p. 25.

character from their circumstances to a presence taking its character from his." [7] To call on the name of the Lord Jesus (Acts 9:14) meant, as its Jewish derivation would suggest, to worship in the Christian community, to approach God through Jesus rather than to petition Jesus alone. As we have already seen from Athanasius, Christians accorded Jesus worship, but he was worshiped in his relation to God. The ancient form of the *Gloria* was: Glory be to the Father, *through* the Son, *in* the Holy Ghost. Jungmann concludes, "Up to the fourth century, the prayer directed to Christ was widely used both privately and in the form of hymns and acclamations. It is not among the official prayers said by the leader of the liturgical assembly. For the latter the rule was the prayer offered to God 'through Christ.' We may say, going beyond this, that the Christians of this early period were conscious of praying to Christ, the head of the Church, as the normal way of praying, because it was the normal way of believing—and so much so that, even in private prayer, a prayer addressed to Christ was regarded as being addressed through Christ to God." [8]

It was the controversy against the Arians, who maintained that Christ was only a creature, which made the Church define more precisely the status of Christ and revise the doxology to assert the equality of the persons of the Godhead. The victory of the Catholics, to which the creed we call Nicene is the great monument, gave

[7] F. J. A. Hort, *The Way the Truth and the Life*, London, 1894, p. 14.
[8] J. A. Jungmann, *The Place of Christ in Liturgical Prayer*, London and Dublin, 1965, pp. 170-71.

impetus to the adoration of Christ. Modern progressive theologians differ in their assessment of Nicaea and the definition of the Council of Chalcedon (451) that Christ is altogether God and altogether man, which was its inevitable sequel. Maurice Wiles thinks that Nicaea "imposed a greater restriction of maneuvering room upon the subsequent theologians than they ought to have been required to accept." [9] David Jenkins argues that it is the affirmation that Jesus Christ is "of one substance with the Father" which, in the categories of its time, safeguards human personality as well as the being and character of God and sets the world free for modern science.

"Transcendence is no necessary bar to immanence, materiality is no necessary bar to spirituality and change and process are no necessary bar to absoluteness and fulfillment. In fact man and the universe fit together because of the involvement of God to that end . . . the definitive fact who is Jesus Christ came to be seen to be the *union* of the transcendent reality of God and the historico-material reality of man without the reduction of the one to the other." [10]

I incline to agree with Jenkins. The resolution of the controversy had strange consequences for Christian devotion. Over the centuries, by directing attention away from the mediatorial role of Christ to his equality with the Father, it presented him as the divine and awful judge, present in the mystery of the

[9] M. F. Wiles, "The Doctrine of Christ in the Patristic Age," in *Christ for Us Today* (Papers from the fiftieth annual Conference of Modern Churchmen 1967), London, 1968, p. 90.

[10] David E. Jenkins, *The Glory of Man*, London, 1967, pp. 48, 49.

altar and the tabernacle, which wretched mortals dared
not approach too often for fear of damnation. In reaction there came the cult of the Virgin and of the
sacred humanity, of the mother and child, and of the
holy name, the five wounds, and, in seventeenth-century
France, the sacred heart.

It is not always understood how all these sentimental
devotions (and I do not use the word pejoratively) are
connected, or how, in their extreme forms, they arise
from an unsatisfactory doctrine of God and of Jesus,
divine and human. They have all enriched Christian
spirituality, have spoken deeply to some hearts and
proved capable of restatement in our own day. Max
Thurian, of the Reformed community of Taizé, has
written a finely eirenical and devotional study of *Mary,
Mother of the Lord, Figure of the Church*, while Karl
Rahner has produced penetrating essays on Marian
themes, and part five of his *Thelogical Investigations*,
volume three, *Theology of the Spiritual Life*, is on
Devotions to the Sacred Heart. Rahner corrects the
unhealthiness and excesses of much popular devotion
to the heart of Jesus, sickly brooding on the ruptured
organ of his human body, and the use of the holy
hour on Fridays to "console" our Lord in his pains
and desolations as though he were still suffering and
we could comfort him as a mother her child. A not
uncomon reaction to Stainer's cantata, *The Crucifixion*,
has been "poor Jesus." This sentimentality has sometimes been compatible with callous and cruel intolerance toward fellow human beings, as Aldous Huxley's
life of Father Joseph, Richelieu's confessor, shows.[11]

[11] Aldous Huxley, *Grey Eminence*, London, 1943.

Almost any devotion can be reformed by a return to scripture and a knowledge of humanity and the condition of the world. A devotional practice gains currency because of a real need inadequately supplied by the official teaching and provision of the Church. It may be deleterious, if not heretical, but, if it has sufficiently captured the imagination, it can usually be rationalized. Nor are these devotions solely Catholic. The treatises of many seventeenth-century Puritans and the hymns of the Wesleys belong to the great tradition which, from the time when the Church became established in society and fixed in dogma, sought, as Dr. Prestige said," to traverse in the opposite direction the road by which Christ ascended into heaven, to return to Golgotha and watch the sacred blood drip to the ground." [12]

Puritan sacramental devotions are medieval in that they urge the worshiper to relate each action of the service to the passion of Christ—the bread itself, wheat cut down and ground and baked, represents not God's bounty and man's toil in creation, but the indignities and buffetings which Christ endured: the breaking of the bread is the rending of his body, the pouring of the wine the spilling of his blood for sinners. In the writings of the Caroline Anglicans there is similar realism, though never degraded by sentimentality or masochism or too much appeal to visual imagination, but dignified, restrained, tender and intensely moving.

[12] G. L. Prestige, *Fathers and Heretics*, London, 1940, p. 377. For an account of Puritan devotion to the passion and the sacred heart see my *Puritan Devotion*, London, 1957, pp. 94–101.

THE CONTINUING CENTURIES 33

Ignatius of Antioch (d. 115) did write in his letter to
the Romans, "My love (Eros) is crucified," and Origen
(c. 185–c. 254) thought that he was referring to Christ.
It is much more likely that he meant "lower-nature,"
or, as Charles Wesley says in one place, "creature-
love" (though elsewhere he takes Origen's view, "My
Lord, my love, is crucified"). Evangelical Christians
would agree with Ignatius Loyola, founder of the
Jesuits, that the contemplation of the crucified should
arouse not only our distress for Jesus in his agony but
our resolve to give ourselves to him who gave his all
to us. The Victorian hymn writer Frances Ridley
Havergal echoes—though doubtless unconsciously—
the *Spiritual Exercises* of Loyola. Compare these lines
from her poem *"Ecce Homo"*:

> *Thou gavst Thyself for me*
> *What have I done for Thee?*
>
> *O let my life be given*
> *My years for Thee be spent*
> *World-fetters all be riven,*
> *And joy with suffering blent!*
> *Thou gavst Thyself to me;*
> *I give myself to Thee.*

with the following Colloquy:

Imagining Christ our Lord present before me on the
Cross, to make a colloquy with Him, asking Him how
it is that being the Creator, He has come to make himself man, and from eternal life has come to temporal
death, and in this manner to die for my sins. Again re-
flecting on myself, ask what I have done for Christ,
what am I doing for Christ, what ought I to do for Christ.
Then beholding Him in such a condition, and thus hang-

ing upon the Cross, to make the reflections which may present themselves.

The mysteries of the Western rosary are similar in style and intention, and it is important to remember that devotions to the Virgin have their origin in devotions to the humanity of Jesus.

Of course, the mystical teachers of the Roman tradition would say that this devotion to the sacred humanity and the passion is but preliminary to the contemplation of God and union with him, a ladder of ascent which perhaps may be kicked away when it is no longer required. Bernard of Clairvaux, whose sermons on the Song of Songs have been so influential in both Catholic and evangelical devotion, speaks sublimely of the holy name of Jesus in words which have been of tremendous influence in hymnody from the Middle Ages to the evangelical revival of the eighteenth century. John Newton's hymn "How Sweet the Name of Jesus Sounds" is perhaps the best-known instance, with its second line from Calvin:

> Jesus! My Shepherd, Husband, Friend
> My Prophet, Priest and King
> My Lord, my Life, my Way my end
> Accept the praise I bring.

Charles Wesley has stanzas which are even closer to Bernard.

But Bernard can also write to the Virgin "O our Sovereign, our Mediatrix, our Advocate reconcile us with thy Son, recommend us to thy Son, present us to thy Son." He seems to have been the first to use the title "Our Lady" and there is a great contrast between

Augustine's sermons for the nativity and his. "Augustine is lost in wonder over the humiliations of the Word; Bernard grows tender over the cries, the frailty and loveableness of the 'Little One, the Desire of all little ones.' " [13] If he were an English Nonconformist minister of the twentieth century, he might well have written of the childhood and youth of Jesus as Leslie Weatherhead has done.

Yet this devotion, in which popular piety may rest, is not intended to be more than the first degree of a love which ends with the beatific vision, which passes from heart to mind and mind to soul, until at last a man loves "not even himself except for the sake of God." [14]

Bernard's spirituality, then, is ultimately theocentric, though much less austere than that of the Spanish mystic John of the Cross. One may say that Bernard sublimates a tender and passionate (though intolerant) nature by meditation on the sacred humanity. John of the Cross, though he uses the language of betrothal and marriage for illumination and final union respectively, does not meditate luxuriously on the life of Jesus. He rigorously eschews all distractions and even brings himself to say (to the horror of Reinhold Niebuhr), "Live in this world as though there were in it but God and thy soul, so that thy heart may be detained by naught that is human." His desire is directed toward God, though, like all Christians, he recognizes "sweetest"

[13] Felix Vernet, *Medieval Spirituality*, p. 93, quoted by Charles Smyth, *The Friendship of Christ*, London, 1945, p. 76.

[14] *De Diligendo Deo* 27, quoted Dom Cuthbert Butler, *Western Mysticism*, 2nd edition, 1926, p. 107.

Jesus as the pioneer and perfector of faith, "the Spouse of Faithful Souls." It is significant that, though a learned man, he seems to have had no books in his cell save the Bible and two treatises of St. Augustine.

It would seem preposterous to introduce at this point a comparison between John of the Cross and Soren Kierkegaard, the sixteenth-century Spanish mystic and the nineteenth-century Danish Lutheran. Yet both were reformers and critics of their established churches and both lived in voluntary detachment from normal human relationships. Above all, both were theocentric and John would have understood Kierkegaard's famous phrase about "the endless yawning (or infinite qualitative) difference between God and man." Indeed he uses the same figure: "How great is the distance there is between all that the creatures are in themselves and that which God is in himself." [15]

Kierkegaard is through and through Christian in his standpoint but he would have found both devotion to the sacred humanity and the examplarism of the liberal Jesus school anathema. He is opposed to a gentle, understandable, acceptable Christianity. It is the absolute which confronts us in the Christ who is always our contemporary. One cannot learn anything about him from profane history. Knowledge gets nowhere; faith in the absolute paradox of God made man alone saves. To reconstruct the details of the life of Jesus is not only impossible; it would be altogether unsatisfactory. It

[15] *The Ascent of Mount Carmel I.* Kierkegaard's sentence is from *Training in Christianity.* Of course the idea is not new to either writer. It is scholastic and the basis of apophatic theology as we have seen, though for both it is a conclusion of religious insight, not of philosophy.

would certainly not give us any assurance on which
to base our hope of eternal life or furnish any proof of
his divinity. "The historical fact that God has existed
in human form is the essence of the matter; the rest
of the historical detail is not even as important as if
we had to do with a human being instead of God. . . . If
the contemporary generation had left behind them
nothing but these words: 'We have believed that in
such and such a year God appeared among us in the
humble figure of a servant, that he lived and taught
in our community and finally died,' it would be more
than enough." [16]

Kierkegaard does not deny historical knowledge to
make room for philosophic speculation about the
mystery of God in Christ. Gossipy historical tradition
he abhorred, as he would the imaginative reconstruc-
tion of the liberals, but any philosophy of substance,
that Jesus Christ is of the actual "stuff" of God, that
divine and human natures were united in the Virgin's
womb, would seem to him none other than an impious prying into wonders too great for mortal man.
His is existential Christology. Christ is no figure of the
past, to be explained as God or as deluded prophet. He
is our contemporary, who confronts us in his very
hiddenness, with the absolute demands of the infinite
God *now*.

Yet Kierkegaard is no mystic. "Mysticism," he
wrote, "has not the patience to wait for God's revelation." Faith waits, waits in the darkness with no light
of reason or of mystic vision; yet it is very bold toward

[16] *Philosophic Fragments*, translated by Swenson, Oxford, 1936,
p. 87.

the infinite God. Kierkegaard's prayers, like Luther's, are completely childlike and open. "Never had it occurred to me to have any hesitation in simply asking God whenever I wanted to enjoy myself, to help and grant me to enjoy myself rightly."

One of the characteristics of developing Christian devotion is then the spirituality which concentrates upon the human Jesus, interpreted often enough according to the needs and fashion of the age. At its most banal, it expresses itself in the evangelical chorus which so affronted Ronald Knox when he heard a party of Sunday school children singing it on the train, "A little talk with Jesus puts it right, all right";[17] or in the child's (or soldier's) declaration "I love Jesus Christ but I hate God." It has inspired the prayer, even the hypnotic entry into ecstatic states, of many thousands who would meditate upon the gospel incidents as if present in the body, or tell the mysteries of the rosary and cry "Jesus! Jesus! Jesus!"; it has been the foundation of the Christianity of those whose life has been an attempt to follow the example of Christ and who, whether subscribing to the creeds or not, have felt themselves haunted by that strange man on a cross.

Others have a devotion which, while it owes everything to the God who revealed himself in Christ and acted decisively for the world's salvation, moves to seek the reality to which the life of Christ points.

[17] R. A. Knox, *Enthusiasm*, Oxford, 1950, p. 570. Since the leader of the party was necking two girls simultaneously, one gathers that the sexual setting was more offensive to him than the ditty.

Sometimes, perhaps, they fail to do justice to the full humanity of Jesus Christ; sometimes they use him as a ladder to mystical experience of God and do not take, with Kierkegaardian or Pascalian seriousness, the fact that he is the way and he alone. They look to Jesus to lead them to the Father and Paul's words, "Even though we have known Christ after the flesh, yet now we know him so no more" (2 Cor. 5:16), are decisive. It is the Christ of faith who matters, not the Jesus of history. They do not encounter him as his first disciples did, either in Galilee or on the Emmaus road. But his living presence (not distinct from that of God himself) is conveyed to them in preaching or prayer or the Eucharist, or in the loneliness of living with nothing but faith.

THE SPIRITUALITY OF WORKS AND THAT OF FAITH

We touched on this distinction in elucidating the New Testament. It corresponds to differences of Christian experience. In the early centuries it may be illustrated by two contemporaries both of whom had tremendous impact on the whole of the Christian future—John Cassian (c. 360–433) and Augustine of Hippo. We choose to consider Cassian rather than Augustine's chief opponent, Pelagius, because this controversy touches more closely the spiritual life. Cassian was a monk, his theology sprang from his quest for holiness and he represents a thoroughly Christian position, which would probably have won the intellectual assent of the majority of serious Christians throughout the ages; whereas Pelagius is little more than a moral rearmer before time.[18]

Cassian belonged to the Eastern tradition of spirituality which conceived of the journey of the soul to goodness as a cooperation between God and human will. But the human will took the initiative. The passions were so overwhelming that they must be rigorously mortified—a process which is impossible without grace, the interior work of God, which is necessary also to save the soul from pride of moral achievement. Grace therefore is the *sine qua non* of holiness and prayer is perhaps its principal means. One of Cassian's most famous passages is on the verse from the Psalms so woven into Christian worship, "O God make speed to save me; O Lord make haste to help me." This is to be the Christian's constant prayer, his meditation, his rebuttal of the tempter, his last words before sleep, his first before work, the final utterance of simplicity before all is lost in God. But in spiritual teaching, grace tended to be assumed and the emphasis was chiefly on human effort, which was necessary to secure grace. "Grace springs from the desire for it."

Cassian thought not so much of original sin, which had man's nature in bondage so that only grace could rescue it, as of a fierce conflict between flesh and spirit in which grace alone could make the spirit prevail. The strife is not itself evil; indeed were there no battle there would be no victory, and so the carnal instincts, against which we must so vigorously war, are not without their good purpose. Cassian also "compared the

[18] For everything on Cassian I am much indebted to Owen Chadwick, *John Cassian*, 2nd ed., Cambridge, 1968.

soul to a feather. If undamaged and dry, the feather is carried up to the sky by a little breath of wind because its nature is so light, but if it is weighed down by damp it cannot move." [19]

All this contradicted the whole experience of Augustine, the brilliant pagan, who had despised Christianity and refused to yield it his mind; the carnal young man, who had prayed for chastity, "but not yet," because the pleasures of indulgence were so delightful. After long hesitation he had given himself to God, but against his natural inclinations and temporal interests. His human will, his own efforts, would never have made him a Christian. Neither did he deserve the mercy of God, for he had chosen to resist it and exulted in his disobedience. All was of grace. "All my hope is in thy exceeding mercy and in that alone. Thou commandest continence; give what thou commandest and command what thou wilt." [20]

This led Augustine to harsh doctrines of original sin and predestination. Man was irretrievably lost in the evil transmitted from Adam of which his fleshly lusts were the dire consequence. Christ is the second Adam who saves us; he died for humanity and God makes his atonement effective only to those whom he elects.

The details of the controversy between Cassian and Augustine need not concern us. The difference between them should not be magnified. In theory both believed that grace was all and that man was utterly dependent on God for salvation. The monk Cassian was afraid

[19] Owen Chadwick, op. cit., p. 114.
[20] Augustine, Confessions, X, 29, quoted by O. Chadwick, op. cit., p. 117.

lest excessive emphasis on grace should lead to moral indolence if not indifference: "Shall we continue in sin that grace may abound?" In practice this was not so, as anyone who reads the moral exhortations of Augustine (or of Paul) will find. Indeed it is ironical that Augustinians, such as the Puritans, devised ethical tests to seek assurance that they had been chosen of God. A *Garden of Spiritual Flowers* (fifth edition 1609), a composite work of five English Puritan divines, lists eight "infallible tokens" of regeneration:

(1) A love to the children of God.
(2) A delight in His word.
(3) Fervent prayer.
(4) Zeal of God's glory.
(5) Denial of ourselves.
(6) Patient bearing of the cross.
(7) Faithfulness in our callings.
(8) Just and conscionable dealings.

William Perkins (1558–1602) besought those who were not conscious of election not to despair or conclude that they were reprobates. Let such a man, he said, "use the word of God and the sacraments, that he may have an inward sense of the power of Christ, drawing him unto him, and an assurance of his redemption by Christ's death and passion."

The paradox is that the Augustinian may have a greater earnestness and confidence in moral effort than a Christian who is less fundamentally pessimistic about human nature, because he depends utterly on the grace of God. He is "confident in self-despair," delivered from the illusion of reliance on his own will and also from anxiety as to the outcome of his struggles and

THE CONTINUING CENTURIES 43

conflicts because his trust is not in himself, who would be bound to fail, but in God's irresistible love. His service is also disinfected from egoism, to use Bremond's phrase, because his reliance on God and his sense of wonder at the overwhelming power of grace and the divine election brings him to worship. The rapturous soliloquy and the spiritual diary are devotional expressions of Augustinianism in its pristine grandeur, as the *Confessions* and the writings of Puritans alike testify.

As Perry Miller has brilliantly shown, Augustinianism, in its Puritan aspect, was one of the chief constituents in the making of the New England mind. Augustine "exerted the greatest single influence upon Puritan thought next to that of the Bible itself, and in reality a greater one than did John Calvin. . . . Some aspects of his work, his defense of the authority of the Church and of the magical efficacy of the sacraments were ignored by the Puritans as by other Protestants," but he is "the archexemplar of a religious frame of mind of which Puritanism is only one instance out of many." [21]

The trouble with any spirituality is that it may become legalistic, its inspiration reduced to logic, the soaring curves of its eagles' flights made a chart for sparrows. This is true not least of those spiritualities which most exalt grace. But it is easy to see that the teachings of a Cassian might develop into an introverted scrupulosity, so that the monastic life became, even when it did not degenerate into privileged worldliness, a constant effort to raise oneself to heaven by one's own

[21] Perry Miller, *The New England Mind: The Seventeenth Century*, Cambridge, p. 4.

shoestrings, and sometimes sins of the flesh gained a greater hold through the efforts spent in fighting them or took an unlovely and violent revenge when it seemed they were subdued.

Cassian was a solitary at heart and it is difficult not to feel that for him perfect love was the flight of the soul to God, of the alone to the alone. His great contemporary the Cappadocian Basil of Caesarea believed in the common life. Christian love "seeketh not its own" and must do more than serve the needs of the individual, while in community gifts and graces may be shared.

Yet even monastic communities became nests of bitterness and corruption. Only the vision of the beauty of holiness and the belief in the divine initiative together with the recognition that this was one of many ways to perfect love and not the supreme course, would rescue monasticism from degenerating into a dreary round of futile self-help. By the sixteenth century it was almost powerless to reform the Church or help it to face the demands of new learning and the new world. But it was monasticism at its best which failed Martin Luther, who was no undisciplined sensualist, yet found that conscientious performance of monastic duties could not give him peace with God. He held the conventional Augustinian doctrines of original sin and predestination but revolted in the power of a warm personal inward religion, the discovery that "He loved me and gave himself for me." His emphasis was more on justification than election. "While we were yet sinners Christ died for us" and through all our lives we never outgrow faith—personal trust in Christ and entire dependence on the merit of his death. This leads us, as it did Kierkegaard, to the outpourings of simple petition and to faith so strong and irrational that prayer is almost magic.

Luther believed that there should be prayer morning and night and that it could well be based on the commandments and the creed. He too felt that company was a much better cure for temptation and aid to godliness than solitude.

Augustinianism had its cruel aspects from the start, but when it was handled by those who had not themselves experienced the irresistibility of grace and made into a Procrustes bed for everyman, it became the tragically narrow system which warped many lives and has given so many novelists their material, most notably Nathaniel Hawthorne's *The Scarlet Letter*.

One of the most fascinating features of Puritanism is its alliance with medieval scholasticism. The schoolmen, of whom the greatest is Thomas Aquinas (c. 1225–74), provided the philosophy of Christendom, a union of biblical faith and its Catholic developments with Aristotelianism. It was in their attempts to provide practical guidance that the Puritans went to the schoolmen, whom Luther and Calvin abominated. The Puritans were clearly excited by the mental agility and logic of these authors but, like the Anglicans Thomas Fuller and Jeremy Taylor, who shared their interest, they compared themselves to the Israelites, who had perforce to sharpen their weapons among the Philistines, since there was no provision in their own resources.[22]

By the seventeenth century, the whole of Protestant-

[22] For a more detailed account I must again refer to my *Puritan Devotion*, pp. 113–24.

ism seems to have been concentrated in Church discipline and practical divinity. The reader of Heinrich Heppe's *Reformed Dogmatics*[23] discovers that the teaching of Calvin is wedded somewhat uneasily to the logic of the schoolmen in more than one contemporary theologian of Switzerland, Holland and Germany. To some extent this Protestant return to medievalism was a counterblast to the new-fangled casuistry of the Jesuits, for whom moral theology tended to be a calculation of minimum requirements, rather than the divine science of holy living, of which the aim was the growth of the Christian in grace.

It was this scholastic moral theology which gave to Puritanism its distinctive conscientiousness. In this it is different from Catholicism, in which conscientiousness tends so often to be scrupulosity, and Lutheranism, in which conscience is the warning voice of God's wrath to be silenced by faith in him who justifies the ungodly, rather than the counseling voice of his guidance. Those of us brought up in the ethos of Puritanism, even in its Methodist form, cannot altogether escape from the power of conscience, perhaps best described in Kant's famous words as "the moral law within." Is not this essential to an understanding of the United States of America? Is not the sense of world mission against communism, typified so notably in John Foster Dulles, a legacy of the Puritan conscience, for which, as Alan Simpson remarks in his

[23] Set out and illustrated from the sources, originally published in German, 1861. English translation by G. T. Thomson, London, 1950.

Puritanism in Old and New England, politics is not the art of reconciliation but a moral crusade?

In the eighteenth century, Puritanism, apart from the survival of the Baxterian tradition in Philip Doddridge, had become a conscience without a heart, narrow, rationalist, lacking in mystique. It was Methodism which revived it. Methodism was Arminian not Calvinist, nearer perhaps to Luther than Augustine (though Wesley did not, I think, fully understand justification in Luther's sense) and a manifestation of enthusiasm, such as only the extreme left-wing, nonscholastic Puritans had countenanced. Methodism was a religion of faith not works, but it insisted that, once the soul was reconciled to God through faith in Christ, the response of good works must follow. Wesley raided the whole store of Christian spirituality to help his followers in the life of prayer and love. He was a spiritual Catholic who found kinship with all who spoke the language of the love of God, whether they were Eastern fathers, Counter-Reformation Romans, Caroline Anglicans, Puritans, nonjurors, Moravians or medieval mystics—though he did not accept any teaching or example uncritically. It is not exorbitant to claim that Wesley unites the best of Augustine and Cassian (though his knowledge of the Eastern fathers may not have included the latter). His was the optimism, not the pessimism, of grace. He taught that holiness is happiness and preached the possibility of Christian perfection. This teaching he derived, without being wholly aware of the fact, from the Byzantine tradition of the Cappadocian fathers, whose differences from

Cassian we have noted above. He thought highly of the homilies of Macarius the Egyptian, whom he regarded as one of the desert fathers. More recent scholarship has established that Macarius was a Syrian monk, whose conception of spirituality derives almost entirely from the Cappadocian Gregory of Nyssa (330–35), brother of Basil of Caesarea, one of the most brilliant philosophers of the fourth-century Church. Macarius and other contemporary writers thought of perfection as a process rather than a state and "gave Wesley a spiritual vision quite different from the static perfectionism envisaged in Roman spiritual theology of the period and the equally static quietism of those Protestants and Catholics whom he deplored as 'the mystic writers.' The Christian Gnostic of Clement of Alexandria became Wesley's model of the ideal Christian. Thus it was that the ancient and Eastern tradition of holiness as *disciplined* love became fused in Wesley's mind with his own Anglican tradition of holiness as *aspiring* love. . . .!" [24] He also, like Basil and Luther, preached a communal not a solitary religion of which, he said, the Bible knows nothing.

> Not in the tombs we pine to dwell
> Not in the dark monastic cell
> By vows and grates confined
> Freely to all ourselves we give,
> Constrained by Jesus' love we live
> The servants of mankind.

For Cassian and the tradition he represents, prayer is the lifting up of the mind to God. This definition first appears in a treatise, *On Prayer*, by a fifth-century

[24] Albert C. Outler, ed., *John Wesley*, New York, 1964, p. 10.

hermit, St. Nilus. This is why Cassian exalts the solitary life which Luther and Wesley found so depressing and so dangerous, and Basil so selfish, and feels that love of neighbor and good works for God's sake may distract from the goal of contemplation.

So much of the Catholic tradition of prayer derives from Cassian of whom the *Rule of St. Benedict* is not the least memorial. It is he who writes of lower levels of prayer, such as penitence, intercession and thanksgiving, which are stages toward "fire prayer," or "pure prayer." This is wordless and completely unselfconscious. Yet it is nourished by scripture and the Psalms are its foundation; in Cassian, they for the first time assume the place they have continued to hold in Christian worship. The way to the beatific vision is through meditation on the incarnate life, even though history and nature also are means by which we may contemplate God. Just as the Puritans thought that the canonical hours of prayer kept the minister from his studies and the layman from glorifying God in his work, and Cranmer reduced the daily offices to two, though with superabundance of scripture, so Cassian felt that the Egyptian custom of two formal offices, morning and evening, was sufficient; the rest of the day should be devoted to private and incessant meditation. But he realized that this might be too severe for some and so describes, in all, five offices which he compares to the five different hours at which the owner of the vineyard in the parable went out to seek laborers. To some extent the offices displaced the Eucharist as the chief acts of public worship for the monks.

Prayer then is contemplation and Augustine would agree. In his quest for the eternal beauty he ceases to be an Augustinian and becomes a Platonist. Indeed it has been claimed by several scholars, though disputed by others, that his mysticism is not entirely Christian, because, as we have seen, it is God centered rather than Jesus centered. He was a true mystic in that he had an immediate apprehension of the glory of God. He had heard that "mysterious strain, melodious and sweet" from the everlasting, perpetual festivity of the house of God. He found the beauty, old yet ever new, more inward than his most inward part and higher than his highest.[25]

Like Cassian, Augustine experienced those states of ecstatic inebriation in which articulate speech failed and there was nothing but silence. Yet his *Confessions*, spiritual autobiography by way of constant conversation with God, are in some measure the prototype of extemporaneous, verbal prayer. The following passage is surely the antecedent of many prayer meetings in chapels and homes which the Bishop of Hippo would have found very strange: "I wrote on the 'fair and fit,' I think two or three books. *Thou knowest, O Lord, for it is gone from me; for I have them not, but they are strayed from me, I know not how.*"[26]

Augustine had such a sense of the presence of God that he could not stop praying. Once he was converted, his intellectual activity was all prayer and often his philosophic speculations were carried on before God.

[25] The last two sentences echo a sermon on Psalm 42 and well-known passages from the *Confessions*.
[26] *Confessions*, Book IV, (XIII), 20. Italics mine.

THE CONTINUING CENTURIES 51

This is thoroughly evangelical—a prayer which breaks
through all forms and, though it may be sustained by
liturgy and dominated by scripture, it overflows set
times and seasons and is coextensive with the whole
of life. Cassian made prayer so by firm discipline and
withdrawal into solitude. This is the monastic, the
Catholic way. Augustine's prayer was the ceaseless outpouring of a heart captured by irresistible love. Though
party distinctions are almost impious in this realm, we
may see in this implacable Catholic the father of the
evangelicals. Perhaps, however, it is the prayer of love,
rather than that of faith. Prayer for Augustine was not
precisely what it was for Luther, who would have en-
dorsed the words of Kierkegaard: "The archimedean
point outside the world is the little chamber where a
true suppliant prays in all sincerity—where he lifts the
world off its hinges." It is Luther who may be deemed
the first of those for whom prayer is not a lifting of
the mind to God so much as a confrontation of wills
—Luther, after the prophets and psalmists and Christ
in Gethsemane.

VERBAL AND VISUAL PIETY

This conflict goes back to the Hebraic roots of
Christianity, to the prohibition of graven images and
the Jewish suspicion of the visual arts in the worship
of God, even though there was something of an in-
consistency here between synagogue and temple. In the
poverty-stricken and proscribed days of the early Church
there was no opportunity for Christians to lavish wealth
on worship and what is now deprecated as triumphal-

ism or Byzantinism was reserved for imperial courts and pagan temples in the first days of the faith. Greater pomp and splendor surrounded the Pope as he became Caesar's successor at Rome and the adoption of some of the panoply of the Byzantine court to elaborate the liturgy may be connected with the reconciliation of pope and Eastern emperor in the seventh century.

Earlier than that, there had been the building of large churches and their costly and sometimes garish adornment. This may have been out of sheer relief at the opportunity Christians now had for public worship, with no fear of punishment, no danger of arrest or death. Christians of many ages and in lands far distant from the Mediterranean have, in their different ways, loved to show their devotion by making their buildings and what went on within them as beautiful as they could, even if they have been planning a meetinghouse rather than a basilica. The ancient world, of course, loved magnificence and surrounded any public act with as much splendor as possible. When Christian worship became public it was natural that it should be attended with at least the glory of civic occasions. And it has been ever thus in the times of establishment, when it has been respectable to be Christian or a certain type of Christian. The chapels of Yorkshire mill owners in the nineteenth century did not want for spaciousness or fine mahogany, many English nonconformist churches of the latter half of Victoria's reign are Gothic revival, while American Methodism has been prolific of *objets d'art* and visual aids in its buildings, not for theological reasons but to help the atmosphere and show that the Church counts in the community; also, doubtless, to give what is best to God.

This urge to erect what Bunyan called "eye-gate" in the house of God has always had its critics and, if one calls them Puritans, it must be remembered that they have not all been Protestants or come into existence since the Reformation. Monks have often found splendid buildings with fine paintings and sculpture a distraction. Augustine was fearful of being lured to temptation by the senses even in church. Jerome disapproved of the replacement of the old sun-baked mud manger at Bethlehem by one of silver. In the desert, the Psalms were often recited by a single voice, while the rest of the monks listened in meditative silence—the Puritan practice of worship which does not like responses, which sees participation as primarily a mental and psychological not physical involvement.[27]

Bernard Manning, in a resplendent passage, has given the theological reasons for this: "To call on the Name of God, to claim the presence of the Son of God, if men truly know and mean what they are doing, is in itself an act so tremendous and full of comfort that any sensuous or artistic heightening of the effect is not so much a painting of the lily as a varnishing of sunlight." [28]

Others have felt that their faith and devotion must be expressed in wood or stone, that the transcendent God does deign to dwell in temples made with hands

[27] Cf. Dom Gregory Dix, *The Shape of the Liturgy*, London, 1945, pp. 304 ff.
[28] Bernard Lord Manning, *The Making of Modern English Religion*, second edition, London, 1968, p. 90.

and that men may be brought to the knowledge of him through sight of

> . . . the high embowed roof
> With antique pillars massy-proof,
> And storied windows richly dight
> Casting a dim religious light [29]

and the appropriately gorgeous and perfectly performed rituals of which these are the setting.

In spite of Augustine, who was as afraid of music in worship, as only a deeply musical person could be, Puritans have usually been more tolerant of this than of the others arts and encouraged congregational singing, which must have brought new life into post-Reformation worship and compensated for the destruction of ornaments and the long lessons and sermons. The ear has not been deemed so distracting as the eye, perhaps because it is easier to concentrate through hearing on one object at once, while the eye may be caught by various delights in turn. There has often been in the Puritan and certainly in the Methodist tradition a vast tolerance of bad music, which has not been thought to do any harm in Church, except by a few condemned as highbrows. (The devil must not be allowed to have all the best, i.e., the most catchy and popular tunes. William Booth would not have said that the devil must not be allowed to have all the best strip shows!) It is significant that the liturgical movement was inspired by Guéranger's desire to recover the Gregorian chant and officially began with a *Moto Proprio* of Pius X for the reform of Church music.

[29] John Milton, Il Penseroso, 1:57–60.

Yet, until the new techniques and restless questionings of our own time, the *word* has been primary in Christian worship and devotion. Karl Rahner, the Jesuit, has written:

For real beauty is the pure appearance of reality as brought about principally in the word. Principally in the word: we have nothing here to say against music. It is too full of mystery. Nevertheless, perhaps lovers of music who are at the same time theologians might give a thought to the fact that God revealed himself in word and not purely in tonal music. But in heaven, they will reply, there reigns the sound of *songs of praise* and not merely the recounting of the glory of God. . . . Be that as it may, the other arts can represent in the first place only what is apprehended and circumscribed. They can set out the images and gestures. . . . But among all the modes of expressing himself that man uses in the arts, the word alone possesses something which is not shared by any other creation of man: it lives in transcendence.[30]

Even sacramental devotion is, properly, a devotion of the word, although of the word visible and objective, not limited by human interpretation, so that Thomas Goodwin, the Puritan, could write of the Lord's Supper:

Many things in a sermon thou understandest not, and haply not many sermons; or if thou doest, yet findest not thy portion in them; but here to be sure thou mayest. Of Sermons, some are for comfort, some to inform, some to excite; but here in the Sacrament is all thou canst expect. Christ is here light, and wisdom and comfort and all to thee. He is here an eye to the blind a foot to the lame; yea everything to everyone.[31]

[30] Karl Rahner, *Theological Investigations*, 3, pp. 301–02.
[31] Thomas Goodwin, *Works*, Edinburgh 1845, p. 408.

Eucharist devotion has sometimes been characterized by excessive realism. Counter-Reformation teaching saw the Eucharist as some kind of a repetition of Calvary, which easily led to speculations about the moment of immolation and a rather carnal piety which regarded the priest's actions as a mime if not a re-enactment of Calvary. Yet the Eucharist is not a passion play and does not, except in Holy Week, include the story of the crucifixion, and then as a part of the liturgy of the word, not of the sacrament. The sacramental wine is, traditionally, not red to simulate blood, but white, and Gerard Manley Hopkins's translation of the "Adoro Te Devote," attributed to St. Thomas Aquinas, gives primacy to the word in the sacrament:

> Seeing, touching, tasting are in thee deceived;
> What says trusty hearing? that shall be believed;
> What God's Son has told me, take for true I do;
> Truth himself speaks truly or there's nothing true.

"Pictures," Gregory the Great is reputed to have said, "are the Bibles of the poor." The age of literacy may be thought to have made them less necessary, which was certainly the Protestant hope. The great missionary-inspired literacy campaigns were undertaken that men and women might be able to read the scriptures, and the last century and a half has seen a prodigious work of Bible translation. Richard Baxter, the great Puritan, says that his father was converted "by the bare reading of the Scriptures in private, without either Preaching or Godly Company, or any other Books but the Bible." That this would happen has

been the hope of many Bible societies, born of the belief that the *word*, printed and read without commentary, might itself speak to non-Christian hearts.
And the daily portion has been part of the evangelical
Christian's rule of life, encouraged since Pius XII in
the Church of Rome. If we are indeed passing from
Marshall McLuhan's typographical to his electronic
age, a good deal more than methods of communication
will need to be thought out anew.[32]

INSTITUTIONALISM AND IMMEDIACY

The fourth contrast is between a spirituality based
on the ordering of life and time in the world around
the commemoration and representation of the gospel
events, and one which demands in various forms a
greater immediacy than even belief in the real presence
of Christ in the sacrament will allow.

From the moment when it was obvious that the
existing world order was not going to be brought to a
speedy end, Christians have had to come to terms with
life in the world. They have had to fight for a place
in human society. The fight has often been hard,
though the establishment of Christianity as the official religion of the Roman Empire under Constantine
in the early fourth century gave the Church a suprem-
acy which, though often assailed and in some lands
overthrown and obliterated, still lingers in the Western
hemisphere. This very recognition of the Church has
brought spiritual problems in its train.

One of the most acute of these, inherited from days

[32] Marshall McLuhan, *The Gutenburg Galaxy*, Toronto, 1962.

long before persecution ceased, though accentuated in a more tolerant world, has been that of the forgiveness of sins and penitential discipline. The New Testament ethic is one for heroes and there are strains in the early writings which imply that, once baptized, a Christian will continue blameless until the Lord comes. The letter to Hebrews has the dire warning "For if we sin wilfully after we have received the knowledge of the truth, there remaineth no more a sacrifice for sins, but a certain fearful expectation of judgment." (10:26) *The Shepherd of Hermas*, a second-century treatise, allows one further opportunity of repentance after Baptism, but no more. As time went on, it was not so much the return of the Lord as the fear of hell which inspired Christian preaching of repentance and made the lapsed willing to submit to the public ordeal of *exomologesis*, rather than remain in their alienation from the Church.

The whole history of Christian spirituality could be written in terms of the tension between rigorism and leniency. The penitential system and the whole of casuistry are attempts to relate the absolute standard of the gospel, Christ's summons to perfection, to the relativities of life in the secular order and to guide and help the Christian to get rid of his sins and to grow in grace. Legalistic, harsh, unimaginative as they have sometimes been, it must not be forgotten that their intention is both realistic and compassionate. Christians are not free from sin from the moment they enter the Christian community. Indeed as they press toward perfection, their temptations may increase and they must be guided with all possible help and sympathy, though at times with a merciful strictness, in living the Christian life. There is no doubt that as time has gone on, and human psychology has been increasingly studied, Christianity has become less rigoristic, until, for some, moral has been replaced by clinical theology.

The classic methods of discipline and guidance have been through the ordained minister, either as exercising the sacramental functions of the priest through the confessional, or, in Protestantism, the godly counsel of the learned divine, given from the pulpit or in the vestry. There have been dangers in post-Tridentine Roman spirituality of penance being thought of more as retribution and punishment than as a strengthening of the soul in the growth toward spiritual maturity.

In the Methodist tradition the substitute for the confessional was the class meeting, the group of no more than a dozen of the committed, who met each week to tell of their experience and their difficulties and to receive the advice of the group, their faults being told "plain and home." This has not survived, though its therapeutic value has been vindicated by modern psychology. But enlightenment in the late eighteenth and nineteenth centuries led to a great relaxation of discipline in the non-Catholic churches. Each man was supposed to be able to find his own way to God and the priesthood of all believers became the slogan of individualism. You do not need to confess your sins to any one except God, nor require any absolution other than his word to the heart. The voice of an informed conscience is the guide to Christian behavior and no one needs any careful instruction in prayer—"you just pray." This did mark a reaction from the sometimes narrow tutelege of priests and directors and is an attitude which not merely survives but is likely to flourish in a time such as our own when there is a rebellion against authority and a casting of doubt on the superior wisdom of the priest or elder.

Another crucial development as the Church adjusted itself to the world was what Dom Gregory Dix described as the "sanctification of time." [33] History succeeded eschatology, the Church looked back to the incarnate life rather than forward to the Saviour who was to come. We must not exaggerate. From the start there had been reminiscences of Jesus and the Eucharist, which recalled him, would clearly fix the minds of worshipers on the events of his passion. As we have seen, the early Christians kept the Jewish hours of prayer, to which were added vigils as they sought to watch for the coming of the Lord. Eschatology meant the sanctification of time, as much as was left of it. But, while the Church was a private society in an alien world, most Christians had only a certain amount of time to give to prayer and worship and they could not always choose their hours of assembly and could not hope to collect the majority of their people for any devotions other than the Eucharist. When persecution ceased, they had increasing opportunities of corporate worship "and gave formal character to one or two of the informal hours of prayer; especially morning prayers (later called Lauds, but then called morning prayers or Matins) and evening prayers, called then *Lucernarium* or lamp-lighting prayers, later called Vespers. In some

[33] See Gregory Dix, *The Shape of the Liturgy*, London, 1945, Chap. XI.

cities these had become established cathedral services
before the end of the fourth century. The laity were
urged to come to morning and evening prayer every
day." [34]

It was monasticism which gradually extended the
hours to the eight of St. Benedict's rule (c. 540), a
discipline which has continued in the life of Catholic
monks and priests ever since, though the second Vatican Council declares that Lauds and Vespers are to be
regarded as "the two hinges on which the Daily Office
turns; hence they are to be considered as the chief
hours." [35] Indeed the changes which the Council prescribes are not dissimilar from those of the English
Reformation, when Cranmer reduced the offices to two
by a masterly synthesis, though he much increased the
readings from scripture. In the Anglican communion
there has remained a hankering after the full scheme
of hours, as is notably instanced in John Cosin's
Private Devotions, first published in 1627 for the benefit of the Anglican ladies in waiting at the court of
Queen Henrietta Maria, who were being shamed by
the much more intense disciplines of the Catholics who
had accompanied Charles I's consort from France.[36]
The book was greeted with howls of Puritan rage as a
subversive instrument of Counter-Reformation, as politically disloyal as it was religiously retrograde. The
tradition however was retained in the Church of England, particularly among the nonjurors after 1689, and

[34] Owen Chadwick, *John Cassian*, pp. 70–71.
[35] *Constitution of the Sacred Liturgy*, 4, 89.
[36] An edition of Cosin's *Private Devotions*, edited by P. G.
Stanwood, with the assistance of Daniel O'Connor, was published at the Clarendon Press, Oxford, December, 1967.

John Wesley, though he did not use Cosin's *Devotions* or the offices for all the canonical hours, had as part of his Oxford rule, which he later republished for Methodists, the repetition of a collect at nine, twelve and three, besides the use of morning and evening prayer, supplemented by long periods of meditation.

The English Reformation, in its more Protestant forms, changed the character of the sanctification of time. Sunday became the Christian's market day, the supreme occasion of public worship and teaching. The other six days were for labor, though they were not thereby to be entirely secular. The book to be compared and contrasted with Cosin's *Devotions* is the work of another Anglican, Lewis Bayly's *The Practice of Piety*. Written about 1610, it reached its twenty-fifth edition by 1630, its fifty-ninth in 1735, and was last reissued in 1842. It was translated into three continental languages and, in 1665, at Cambridge, Massachusetts, into the tongue of the local Indians. Thoroughly Calvinist, this manual prescribes a devotional discipline for the then new merchant class, the heads of large households and men of trade. The *Book of Common Prayer* is presupposed but, whereas for Cosin its complement is a reformed breviary, for Bayly the extra devotions are not set offices but compositions which could serve as a model for extemporaneous prayers. They are long and theological, verbose in comparison with Cosin. Bayly expects the Bible to be read through in the course of the year and shows how this may be done—three chapters a day and the *Prayer Book* Psalms. But we must not be misled into thinking that Bayly's style of devotion came into existence with the reformers, whereas Cosin is Catholic. Though *The Practice of Piety* is much more a handbook of theology for laymen than any medieval primer, Bayly, like other English Puritans and the later German pietists whom they influenced, borrows a scheme of recollection from the Spanish humanist Ludovicus Vives (1492–1540), who came to England in 1523 as tutor to Princess, later Queen, Mary. The simple tasks and occasions of daily life must be associated with the events of the gospel and the great ends of providence. The bed is always to remind the sleeper of his grave, his rising of the resurrection from the dead. Should he hear the cock crow, he must remember Peter's denial and penitence with many tears. The putting on of clothes is to carry the mind back to man's primeval innocence and fallen shame. The sun streaming through the windows is to be a sign of the sun of righteousness, risen with healing in his wings.

The other aspect of the sanctification of time was the establishment of the Christian year. This was secured in main outline by the end of the fourth century. "As the daily devotions of Christians hallowed the beginning and ending of each day, so the liturgical year sanctified the annual cycle of the seasons. Through all the Christian centuries this structure has remained, protecting and ennobling the Church's worship." [37]

The importance of this cannot be overestimated, though it had its dangers. In the Middle Ages there was an appalling proliferation of saints' days and feasts of the Virgin, but even apart from these excesses, the

[37] A. A. McArthur, *The Evolution of the Christian Year*, London, 1953.

Christian year breaks up the unity of commemoration, isolates the gospel events from one another and fosters what the reformers would have called history faith rather than saving faith. In some teaching and devotion based upon it, there is a pietistic and overimaginative lingering in the shadows of the gospel narratives and a failure to relate them to the whole design of God's mercy. There may also be a lack of immediacy against which mystics of all kinds as well as adventists and evangelicals protest. There may be overmuch commemoration and a dearth of present experience and future hope.

The Catholic Christian and the Lutheran, Anglican and Reformed find immediacy in the sacrament of Holy Communion of which, it is now recognized, preaching should form a part. The medieval dogma of transubstantiation is an attempt to explain this real presence in spatial, quasi-material terms, but the Roman Catholic theologians of the liturgical movement, such as the Benedictine Dom Odo Casel, followed by the Lutheran Rudolf Otto, the Anglican Gregory Dix and the Congregationalist C. H. Dodd, see the miracle not in space but in time, not in substance but in event. In the Eucharist we become the contemporaries of all the mighty acts of God in Christ. We are there "in the night in which he was betrayed, at Golgotha, before the empty tomb on Easter Day, and in the upper room when he appeared; and we are at the moment of his coming, with angels and archangels and all the company of heaven, in the twinkling of an eye at the last trump." [38]

[38] C. H. Dodd, *History and the Gospel*, Cambridge, p. 234.

This, however, would not satisfy many Christians. The original Quaker protest against sacramentalism was not so much to assert that all life is sacramental as to insist on inward reality as against outward form. To eat in remembrance of Christ's death is not enough; as George Fox writes in his *Journal*, we must come into his death and die with him. Fox uses richly sacramental language, but he feels that to rely on ordinances is to live as though the Holy Spirit had not been given, to remain with the partial when the perfect has come. Similarly, some Friends felt that times and seasons set apart for prayer were a second best. If Christ is in the heart then prayer is a perpetual state.

THE SPIRITUALITY OF PROTEST

This has already brought us to mention one of the many movements of intense Christianity which have not found a home with the orthodox confessions and which hold the ecumenical movement suspect lest the unity of all Christian people should fetter the spirit. Another of the strongest and most valid criticisms of ecumenism is that it seeks to anticipate by human organization and contrivance the day of God, that like belief in the real presence in the Eucharist, it may deny the *parousia*, the coming of Christ in God's time. This is why adventists and some reformed are bound to oppose it. Yet another criticism is that the result may be conformism, without the dialectic of protest.

Throughout Church history there have been those who have reacted against "the establishment" in the interests of a living faith. There were the Montanists, in the second and third centuries, ecstatic, enthusiastic, claiming the spirit of prophecy and living by an austere, unworldly discipline. There is a mystic underworld, persecuted and derided for the most part, in danger of heretical excess if not blasphemy, yet bearing witness both to the failure of Christendom and the evangelical beatitude of poverty. Until the Reformation set the scriptures free, much of the spiritual rebellion against the evils of the Church was mystical in temper, most of the reforming movements sought to recall Christians to the inward religion of love sometimes aided by the contemplation of God in the outward world of nature in reaction from his imprisonment in relic-filled shrines and hierarchical systems. Neither did the Reformation mean an end of such manifestations. For many, the orthodoxies of Luther and Calvin were but old tyrannies in different guise.

The success of communism in Eastern Europe has meant the rehabilitation of Thomas Müntzer (1491–1525), whom Luther did not hesitate to call an archdevil. Müntzer was a revolutionary, anticlerical and violent, the Stokley Carmichael of Protestantism. Yet he had a deep devotion and as a liturgist may be compared with Thomas Cranmer, some of whose work he anticipated, notably the reduction of the choir offices to two and a vernacular Mass. He belongs in part to the German mystical tradition of Eckhart, Tauler and Suso and also to the modern devotion, represented by "The Imitation of Christ." Later he became something of an enthusiast, believing in direct inspiration and placing great faith in visions and dreams. What began and continued in mysticism ended in politics, the politics of revolution.

But though his deeds did not rival Müntzer's, nor had his theology anything in common, the prince of protesters is undoubtedly Kierkegaard. In the last months of his life he wrote a series of articles which have been collected in our own time as his *Attack upon "Christendom."* They were provoked by a panegyric he heard upon the primate of all Denmark, who had been a good man and a good bishop, but not, in Kierkegaard's judgment, an apostle. Thus he contrasts, by the most vigorous and at times brutal satire and invective, the establishment Lutheranism of his native land with the religion of the New Testament. Baptism, the lord's supper, Confirmation, marriage have become seemly social conventions, used by men and women and priests who have no understanding of the scandal of the gospel, no intention of living the life of Christ and his apostles.

The worldly young man, without a thought of God, presents his child for Baptism and a pretty ceremony is performed with solemn promises made by godparents who have no idea how to keep them. Yet "it was with this sacred ceremony the Saviour of the world was consecrated for his life's work, and after him the disciples, men who had well reached the age of discretion and who then, dead to this life . . . promised to be willing to live as sacrificed men in this world of falsehood and evil."

Three or four times a year a tradesman, whose honest statement of his creed would be "Every man's a thief in his business," goes to communion, and then back to his usual way of life in which getting and spending alone matter.

And this is what one dares to offer to God under the name of the Sacrament of the Lord's Supper, the Communion in Christ's body and blood!

The Sacrament of the Lord's Supper! It was at the Last Supper that Christ, Who from eternity had been consecrated to be the Sacrifice, met for the last time before His death with His disciples, who also were consecrated to death or to the possibility of death, if they truly followed Him. Hence for all the festal solemnity it is so shudderingly true, what is said about His body and blood, about this blood-covenant which has united the Sacrifice with His few faithful—blood-witnesses, as they surely were willing to be.[39]

By the standards of established Christianity the New Testament is no longer truth. "When all are Christians, Christianity *eo ipso* does not exist." The spiritual man is able to endure the paradox of Christianity, the offense of the cross, isolation and unpopularity. But Christendom means conformity, being well-liked, sharing the accepted views of sensible men, being in no sense fanatical, ignoring the hard sayings of Christ.

Let us take an example. In "Christendom" this is what Christianity is: a man with a woman on his arm steps up to the altar, where a smart silken priest, half educated in the poets, half in the New Testament, delivers an address half erotic, half Christian—a wedding ceremony. This is what Christianity is in "Christendom." The Christianity of the New Testament would be: in case that man were

[39] Soren Kierkegaard, *Attack Upon "Christendom,"* translated by Walter Lowrie, Princeton University Press, 1944.

really able to love in such a way that the girl was the
only one he loved and one whom he loved with the whole
passion of a soul (yet such men as this are no longer to be
found), then, hating himself and the loved one, to let her
go in order to love God. And it is in view of this I say
that such men of such quality and caliber, are not born
any more.[40]

Kierkegaard writes outrageously and from his own
warped experience. To the last passage many would re-
tort that marriage could make more exacting and sacrificial demands and be a truer way of loving God than
celibacy. Modern spirituality has not made up its mind
as to whether Kierkegaard is right or wrong. But it
tends to canonize the men of protest.

Some Common Assumptions

It will be clear that from the long story of the
centuries certain basic assumptions are common to all
the diverse forms of spirituality:

(1) In control of our destinies is a personal God.
Personality does not exhaust his being, but he is, as
Martin Buber said, "addressed, not expressed." Sometimes words are used to ask God to intervene in human
affairs or even to change his proximate will; sometimes they are but the ladder of ascent to a communion
which is beyond all speech, all thought and all human
relationships. Sometimes prayer is to be the vehicle of
God's action in the world; sometimes it is, principally,
the means whereby the individual is united to God.
But the unique and determinative relationship of man's

[40] Kierkegaard, *op. cit.*

life is with God. We fulfill the end for which we were born only as we are in union with him, though the union is sometimes conceived of as active cooperation in partnership with other Christians, sometimes as absorption in the Godhead, though without loss of our own personal identity.

(2) The way to God is through Jesus Christ our Lord. Again this unanimity is varied by differences of understanding and emphasis. Jesus is the mediator, but whether because of his victory over evil powers, his provision, through his sacrificial death, of a remedy for the defilement of sin, or our response to his example of love, depends on cultural background and temperamental inclination. Again, for some Christians, Jesus is the one who leads us to God; for others the whole of devotion seems concentrated upon him; he is God for them.

(3) Human nature has an earthly and a godward aspect. Originally, the soul meant the unique essential life of a man, his whole being of embodied mind. But conventionally it has described the part, naturally immortal, which is yet in the grip of death and must be saved by being brought into relation with the life of Christ. How this happens and what are its consequences, are questions which lead to the diverse answers of the different Christian spiritualities, but the basis of them all is the existence of the soul of man.

(4) There is a Christian presence in the world. This is the perpetual witness to the Christ event. Through its continuous and corporate memory we know the things concerning Jesus, and it is the school of holiness, the help and support of the wayfaring Christian. There

have been grave disagreements about the nature and authority of this presence. Is it a hierarchical and fundamentally unchanging institution or a fellowship of believers? Must the individual regard it as a supreme authority with which he must live in closest association, or is it a gentle influence, not at all oppressive, in the background of a man's search for God? And in which of its many manifestations is authentic Christianity to be found, or does it linger in almost every form, though sometimes obscured by irrelevancy and corruption? Yet, through the ages, there have been few who would deny that in some sense the Church is necessary to the Christian way.

These, then, have been the presuppositions of all schools of Christian spirituality, even the most heterodox. Each of them is challenged by the cultural revolution of our time, which makes many Christians convinced that the old patterns of prayer and discipline are outmoded beyond recovery, not only because of sociological change, but because their underlying philosophy is no longer credible. To this we must now turn.

PART II

The World of Today

3 Spirituality and Contemporary Society

It is easy to be deceived into exaggerating the extent to which Christians themselves are aware of the uncongenial climate of the second half of the twentieth century. The present decade has seen a recession within Protestant and Catholic communions throughout the Western world, but sects and campaigns draw vast crowds, while, naturally, the decline has been more noticeable in centers where the churches were already weak than in the more affluent towns and suburbs. Much of the numerical strength and social effectiveness that remains is conservative. The majority of churchgoers, even some who in their secular lives are initiators of radical reorganization, feel that the Church should be an ark of security in a restless and unstable world. They are prepared to oppose change even when it is advocated as a return to the authentic tradition. Many devout Roman Catholics are bewildered by the liturgical reforms of the second Vatican Council and think that the impregnable rock is being worn away by the battering tides of modernism. When they are told that the changes are in accordance with primitive, perhaps apostolic, practice they are not comforted. Many Protestants still find Norman Vincent Peale a sure guide and for them the problem of prayer is solved

75

when it is seen simply as a help to a happy and integrated personal life. Their position is no different from Frank Sinatra's: "I'm for anything that gets you through the night—booze or religion," except, of course, that they opt for the "respectable" alternative. They are impatient of theology. Worship ordered on the principles of Cranmer, Calvin or Wesley is condemned as alien or unintelligible.

There are also those who see in Christianity not so much a religion of personal help or other-worldly consolation as a defense of the political and social *status quo*. It is the chief bulwark against communism, and conversion to Christ leads to social conformity. The beatnik has his hair cut and becomes a disciplined soldier. The hippy is made into a responsible suburban wife and mother. The Negro eschews violence and settles down to work for his employer.

THE INTELLECTUAL REVOLUTION

All this completely ignores the revolution in thought which began two hundred years ago and is now seen victorious in the whole of the culture of the Western hemisphere. At the risk of over simplification, we may say that this may be described as the triumph of empiricism. Life is no longer regarded as the working out of certain fixed principles eternal in the heavens, a deduction for individuals and societies from an everlasting "given." Nothing is to be taken for granted; everything must be approached with an open and questioning mind. If we are trammelled by accepted presuppositions we shall misread the signs of the universe.

We shall impose our own mental pattern on the scheme of things and discovery will be impeded.

This is very different from traditional Christianity whether in its Hebraic or Greek forms. "In the beginning God . . ." is the opening verse of the Bible and this was easily wedded to Platonic idealism, to the belief in forms laid up in heaven and time as the moving image of eternity. It was when the organizing power of the human mind and its ability to order the universe according to its own predilections was fully realized that faith in preestablished harmonies was shaken. What if they were man made and did not necessarily correspond to objective reality? What if man's mind was caught in a vicious circle of presuppositions which it claimed to deduce from the evidence but which were in fact its own constructions, imposed on phenomena and inhibiting free inquiry? Openness certainly leads to scientific advance. Must we not, in all realms, live by what we discover in experience, not by fixed principles?

This is a very crude account of the new way of thinking. It is obvious that, taken to its logical conclusion, this understanding of the mind would prove that objective reasoning is impossible and that we are going to pour our experience into our own mental mold whether we believe in eternal axioms or not. Alan Richardson states the matter by use of another, more vivid metaphor:

One of the perennial illusions of the rationalist mind is that, because one is not an Anglican or a Presbyterian, not a Christian or a Marxist, and so on, one is therefore "impartial." We cannot see our own ideological spectacles, and because our eyes are protected by them, we do not notice that as we throw our sand against the wind, the wind blows it back again.[1]

But when this is admitted the result could be complete skepticism. It is possible to see through everything, even rationalism, and conclude that there is no truth, no ultimate reality, simply a series of impressions of the material world outside ourselves which cannot be made into a system and which we must forever check and countercheck against other observations. The nearest we can come to certainty is in our investigations of the physical universe (of which the life of man is part) but even this is but provisional, not absolute, and if it were deemed absolute no further progress would be possible.

This is, roughly, the scientific approach. If the textbook says that the result of mixing two liquids should be a pink solution and, after repeated and accurate experiment the solution is persistently brown, the chemist does not say "I have erred. I do not understand how, but, clearly, I am going against the testimony of the elders and the written word and the eternal order and must be wrong." He rewrites the textbook.[2]

Skepticism and impiety (in the literal sense of not being inhibited by respect for the traditions of one's predecessors) have led to the advance of science and it is no wonder that the spirit of the age is inimical to authority of all kinds, whether of imagined superiors

[1] Alan Richardson, History, Sacred and Profane, London, 1964, p. 101.

[2] I have borrowed and adapted here an illustration from John Wren-Lewis, but I am not aware that it is found in any of his published papers.

on earth or of an almighty controller of the universe in heaven. The way to conquer cholera is not to believe that it is the mysterious visitation of an offended deity who must be besought to stay his hand, possibly by being reminded of the sacrifice of his Son, but by ruthless and courageous examination of the epidemic, isolation of the germ and preventative measures in the future. It is not prayer that we need, but disinfectants; the problem is not one of deity but of drains.

If one wants rain to save a people from famine, or sunshine for a happy vacation, to ask God gives results which any statistical tests would show to be random in the extreme. Sometimes the prayers are answered, sometimes not, in neither case for any apparent reason, though guilty conscience or complacent self-satisfaction could devise one. It would seem better to study the forecasts and the phenomena and work toward human mastery of the elements, so that the desert may blossom as the rose or fine weather be contrived when people need it.

And if this is true in nature, may it not also apply to human nature? Will not the techniques which have succeeded in the physical sciences help us with the life of man? Already this is happening. Psychology, sociology, biochemistry are regnant, and personality can be changed more easily than the weather, and prophets hail the day when we shall be able to produce the types we want.

No study has been more influenced by the intellectual revolution than that of history. This is of particular importance for the Christian faith, which has often triumphantly claimed that it is based not on speculations of philosophy but on events which happened. In our own century, historians have come to see that it is impossible to disentangle facts from interpretations, or to arrive at objective assessments of what really happened once one tries to penetrate the surface of brute physical circumstances. The American Carl Becker went so far as to say, in 1910, "The facts of history do not exist for any historian until he creates them, and into every fact that he creates some part of his individual experience must enter." [3] The so-called facts of our redemption, then, are the creation of the men who recorded them; other interpretations of Jesus are possible from those in the New Testament and the task of establishing the truth is more complicated than the simple believer realizes. It is possible only out of the clash of many differing interpretations.

But this is not all. The study of an event is not only a matter of the historian creating his own facts. He has to do this through the interpretations of his predecessors. And this involves the process of stripping down, until what he sees may be a nude, divested of the panoply of the hagiographers, or those who worked with the presuppositions of a different age. The story of the emperor's new clothes is pertinent. What the wily tailors had offered the emperor as a gorgeous robe, was hailed as such by the gullible populace, but was seen by the small boy to be nakedness. So it could be with Christianity. Behind the veneration of the centuries does there lie more than the career of a strolling preacher

[3] Quoted from Becker's article on "Detachment and the Writing of History," in *Atlantic Monthy*, by Alan Richardson, *op. cit.*, p. 192.

about whose grisly death there was some kind of mystery? This led his followers into a cult, which partly fortuitously, partly because of its intrinsic appeal at that time, managed to become the dominant religion and heir of the declining Roman Empire. Is there more to it than that? We may dismiss such reductionism as preposterously inadequate to account for what the historical consensus would accept. But at the very least, the old certainty has gone.

Similarly the 'religious consciousness' is subjective and related to its social period. In consequence it is seen not so much as the awareness of God, implanted by him who has made us for himself and whose voice speaks summoning us to his service, as the product of sociological conditions, which is likely to change with these conditions and possibly to disappear as the life of communities is sustained more and more by the empirical world alone.

Such authority as produces results which lead to human well-being, life, liberty and the pursuit of happiness, would seem to reside in groups rather than individuals, and—if the well-worn figure be allowed—to be horizontal rather than vertical. As we proceed in partnership along the winding and perilous road of human history, we make discoveries which we test by each other's insights and continuing experience and may thus achieve greater control over recalcitrant nature. But no angel with a flaming sword must keep us from any supposed garden of God.

In the Western world there are few leaders. Politicians may be exalted for a while but are vilified with amazing speed thanks to the mass media, so that reputations are lost within a matter of weeks as is seen in the cases of President Johnson in the U.S.A. and Prime Minister Wilson in Great Britain. Pop stars are revivalists without religion and have inherited something of the power of the orator or preacher of former days. But they are not directed toward changing the world and are not followed in any cause save that of mass entertainment. Since they are not religious or political figures with moral responsibilities, it does not much matter what kind of people they are and whether they are drug addicts or evangelical Christians does not seem to affect their popularity or to impress their fans.

The person who has been most downgraded in society is the father. The emancipation of women and the increasing triumph of sex equality—a consequence of rationalism—have taken away much of the mystique of the male. The father has had to leave the secluded eminence of study or armchair to help with the dishes. He is much more the man about the house, daddy rather than father, and often wins respect and love not because of his remoteness but because he is accessible, the helpmate of his wife, the playmate of his children. This would seem entirely beneficial, but it blurs fatherhood so that the man of the house is part father, part elder brother, while the status of motherhood remains unassailable, so far, because of the unique intimacy of physiological relationship.

The results of this for religion are obvious. The image of God as father, even though Jesus called him *Abba*, daddy, is not so powerful in our world as of old. The concept is by no means empty. Indeed it is not the fatherhood of God but the whole article of belief in a supreme controlling personality which causes the trouble. Even so, fatherhood may be assailed as tending either to an authoritarianism which is outmoded or a sentimentality which is nauseating, while, insofar as the male principle is dominant and there is no doctrine of the motherhood of God, the Christian analogy is being drawn from only a part of human experience and perhaps the less significant part.

To sum up: the intellectual revolution to date means that as citizens of the later twentieth-century Western world, we live in an age in which there is no infallible unchallengeable authority, no public philosophy, no tradition unviolated by criticism. Miracles as interventions in human affairs by a supreme being cannot be objectively verified and if there is any reality whom we may address as God, he does not answer prayer in any sense analogous to our use of that verb in human affairs. Our only hope is in ourselves, working together. Our only authority the imperfect, tentative mind of the group.

THE TECHNOLOGICAL REVOLUTION

Empiricism, setting man free from ancient presuppositions and inhibitions about interfering with nature, has resulted in technology, man's control over his environment and power to change it on a scale more lavish than ever before. A person who has lived from the year 1890 has seen more outward change than has occurred in any previous period of history. The speed of change is increasing all the time so that reforms of any kind in any organization may be outdated and irrelevant almost before they are made. It is very difficult for legislation either in state or church to do more than attempt a shuffling and ludicrous dance to the ever-varying and yet more furious rhythms of the *zeitgeist*. The temptation to sink back into the familiar and conventional is almost irresistible even though this is, in fact, to wait for death.

Technology has affected man's awareness of reality. In the large cities of Western Europe, Gothic spires no longer outsoar all other buildings. They are reduced to size, as they always have been in Manhattan, by multistoried palaces of trade or dwellings, luxurious or humble. This means that though men may still be overwhelmed by the marvels of human construction this is no longer related to religious worship. In any case psychology has debunked the spire into a phallic symbol, but the unsophisticated, innocent of Freud, are nevertheless less likely to find sermons in stones than were their ancestors.

Of course, this is not so inimical to worship as it may at first thought seem. Harvey Cox, in a penetrating essay on "The Restoration of a Sense of Place," borrows Constantinos Doxiadis's notion of "the human scale." This is "the essential dimension of any city." To desert Cox, for a moment, we could maintain that, in terms of this, an ancient cathedral, even from the outside, has a dimension which cannot be measured in feet, while within there is no rivalry from skyscrapers. Such is the architect's magic, that a comparatively small area may give the sense of vastness and of the transcendent. Also, to return to Cox, technology may make possible new experiences of the immensity of space. Cox quotes Jean C. Rowan:

Today we have many spatial experiences that did not exist before. Air travel, for instance. After a jet flight among the clouds, can one be really stirred by the architectural space within the terminal building? Or, assuming that there is a church on top of a skyscraper, how will a worshipper react to it after a thrilling ride up into the sky in a glazed, exterior elevator? Is looking down 500 feet from an upper floor of a high-rise tower a greater spatial experience than looking up 100 feet at a domed ceiling? And in the not-too-distant future, when man will be floating through the vast spaces of the celestial void, how will he react to earth's puny architectural spaces, however great they might be in the traditional sense?[4]

Cox, of course, is not really concerned about any supposed numinous or religious sense. All that matters for him is that man has a place in which to be man. God, as St. Paul says, "has no need of temples of wood or stone"! This, to my mind, is misguided, since I do not think that man can be truly man without the awareness of God, at least on the part of some people, and therefore I believe that man's sense of place should like his other senses, as well as his extra-sensory perceptions, lead him to the transcendent. Our technological age appears to militate against this, but not inevitably. Old holy places may still remain and new ones may be added, less localized because the human scale is vaster, thanks to man's conquest of the universe.

Yet whenever outer space is mentioned, one remembers the Russian astronaut's laughing confession of his failure to find God. Gabriel Fackre has told of two, presumably American, astronauts who had returned from

---

[4] Harvey Cox, *On Not Leaving It to the Snake*, New York, 1967, p. 123, cited from Jean C. Rowan, *Progressive Architecture*, June 1965, p. 139.

a record-breaking flight, in the midst of which there had been an engine failure which had forced them down prematurely. One journalist asked, "Did you feel closer to God during all the trouble?" The spaceman who had been answering most of the questions preferred to pass this to his colleague who, embarrassed, blurted out, "We were busy." Fackre goes on:

. . . the theological student who graduates from the seminary these days is too much part of the new world to deny the facts of life. He has stood in a European airport terminal on a Sunday morning and seen the thousands of people who are not in the pew—because they are racing hither and yon in all of the new secular exhilaration and anguish of our day. And he may even be honest enough to have noticed with Walter Kaufman that the most rural congregation does not rest its safety in the hands of prayer, but puts a very worldly object on top of its steeple to take care of lightening bolts—a lightening rod. There is really not much difference between the astronauts and St. John's-by-the-Cornfield, for both turn to human gadjets in time of peril.[5]

So many of the powers once ascribed to God have now been given to men. And this seems true even of the final solution of this world's affairs. As John Burnaby wrote, "We have learned to face the possibility that human decisions based on knowledge of the properties of matter may bring upon the world a cataclysm once supposed to be at the sole disposal of the Almighty."[6]

[5] Gabriel Fackre, Baccalaureate Sermon, Lancaster Theological Seminary, May 29, 1966, printed in *The Preacher's Quarterly*, December 1966, pp. 273–74.
[6] John Burnaby, "Christian Prayer," in *Soundings: Essays Concerning Christian Understanding*, edited by A. R. Vidler, Cambridge, 1962, p. 232.

Other consequences of technology are less apocalyptic but just as revolutionary. We cannot yet tell what will be the effect of the mass media on man's perceptions and mentality. It would seem that he will tend more and more to think pictorially—visually rather than verbally—and that his mind will work less by old-fashioned logical progression—from premisses to a conclusion—and more by vivid impressions. Contrast a formal sermon or lecture with a television documentary or play. The preacher or lecturer engages his auditors in a kind of meditation, leading them step by step, point by point, to his desired end. It is very much the classic spiritual technique. But the TV producer does not always stick even to chronological order. There are flashes and flash backs, all brief. We do not stay anywhere long enough to reach a conclusion or to see a situation through to its end. The program may finish inconclusively. Pictures have replaced argument. The technique, in Marshall McLuhan's phrase, is that of "the suspended judgment." Visual sequence becomes the rational norm and art is handed over to the unconscious.[7] Discursive reasoning is subordinated to something more like contemplation.

Similarly the written word no longer has its ancient power, although TV programs have driven some men to their libraries, their intellectual appetites whetted. Also, more ordinary people are reading about religion through paperbacks and magazine articles, though in secular publications these rarely give the orthodox Christian party line. There would seem to be no substi-

[7] Compare Marshall McLuhan, *The Gutenberg Galaxy*, Toronto 1962, p. 278.

tute for the word in fully human existence, for it is this which makes possible genuine personal encounter as well as true individuality. Meanwhile, as McLuhan says, we live in the trauma and tension of conflicting technologies and awareness. The one simple certainty is that, for the mass man, what is *seen* will assume ever greater importance over what is heard or read.

The Church is becoming gradually aware of this. But in its ordered life, its service books, its pastoral guidance and its theology, it is still too often organized for a rural rather than an urban or industrial society. It has not completely caught up with the first industrial revolution, let alone the second, and is not altogether living in the typographical let alone the electronic age. The old Christian pattern of Sunday as the great day of rest or of celebration, of the hours of day and night divided between work, recreation and sleep, with the assumption of regular periods of prayer and perhaps the saying of offices is broken by shift work and automation. The sanctification of time cannot be for us as it has been throughout the Christian centuries. We may soon approach an era in which we shall ask of our friends "Have you had your Sunday this week?"

Where Sunday is not a working day through shifts, the service industries, entertainment or war, it is the day of the family, and may be spent in a variety of ways from outings to the beach or countryside, visits to friends or odd jobs around the house or garden. In the more prosperous communities, a large minority if not the majority may devote the morning to church as a seemly social custom, supremely respectable and con-formist and calculated to give the children some grounding in accepted morality and cultural norms. But there are few who live the liturgical life, whose thought and time are dominated by the reenactment of the Christian story and its relation to their seven weekly attempts at living, and even less whose churchgoing has a prophetic relation to society. This is due to some extent to the self-contained nature of urban life, with its supermarkets and stores, which make regular visits to town unnecessary for the housewife, while the commuter does not become personally and socially involved with the district in which he does his daily work, but escapes each night to be with his family and friends. In America the isolation of suburb from city is assisted by vast networks of local radio and newspapers, which, until events in the world and nation assumed such horrific proportions, meant that it was possible to live in a fairly affluent community without much awareness of the problems outside.

The family still survives, though it is rarely, as the Puritans hoped, a little church with its own regular worship. The blare of the radio, the diverse preoccupations of the growing children and their embarrassment at the exposure of religious intimacies (unless they are evangelicals) militates against this. It is a smaller unit than in the days of domestics and retainers and, as we have already mentioned, the father is not any more its undisputed, dictatorial head. The family remains formidable and often ousts all other groups as the center of interest for its members. Yet the ties of kinship can wear surprisingly thin and the fact that women are now emancipated and so many of them find marriage and motherhood compatible with an independent career, though it can bring a healthy new freedom into marital relations, may also endanger fidelity and the security of the home. Horst Symanowski has succinctly expressed this, among other changes:

At the marriage altar the pastor still says the beautiful old words about the woman being made as man's helper— and, indeed, he means *this* woman of *this* man now before him. But doesn't the pastor know that after the honeymoon this man will work days on end with other girls and women and that this woman will work with entirely different men? What should he say to them at their wedding in view of this situation? It is astonishing that so many marriages still endure despite these circumstances. . . . But we should also recognize that a lot more love and a good deal more strength is needed in married life today than was needed in times when the wife brought a few acres of land and a few cows with her into the marriage thus setting up a "partnership" that could not thereafter be dissolved.[8]

In spite of the remaining isolation of some social units, the greatest consequence of modern technology is to make this one world a spaceship in which we are all traveling together and from which there is no escape. We are in no sense detached from anything that happens anywhere on the globe and no man, no society of men, is an island. The most unrealistic and disastrous policy for any nation to pursue, or any church, would be isolationism.

This means not only that spirituality cannot avoid being ecumenical, it means that other religions are likely to be of increasing importance to Christianity. America has always been in some sense an international, multi-

[8] Horst Symanowski, *The Christian Witness in an Industrial Society*, London, 1966, p. 45.

racial society and in the great conurbations, religions have lived cheek-by-jowl, and no one of them has been established. Yet there is now an increasing sensitiveness on the part of Christians to other faiths as instanced by the second Vatican Council's famous constitution *Lumen Gentium*. Some Christians, indeed, wonder whether there is any point in seeking the conversion of adherents of the other great religions and the crusading spirit is largely dead.

Yet it is in other ways that this encounter may influence spirituality. To some extent it has always done so, since the Church has the Jewish scriptures. The frontiers of Orthodoxy march with those of Eastern religions and in some teaching the Jesus prayer is related to the mysticism of the Sufis. But each Holy Week the stories of the passion are read with increasing embarrassment as it is realized how the evangelists in the interests of the gentile mission exonerate Pilate and blacken the Jews, while at Easter, the narrative of the passover, of such great typological significance, seems to hallow the enmity between Israel and Egypt, which the contemporary situation in the Middle East forbids us to exacerbate. No longer dare the Church pray for "Jews, Turks, infidels and heretics." Talk of "the heathen" does not help the peace of the world.

THE UPSURGE OF PROTEST

So far we have ignored the smoldering scrap heap of the new world of technology. It is far from being all drains and laboratories, light and air-conditioned office blocks, computers, refrigerators and subtopian amenities. There is "downtown." The squalor and dreariness beyond the park, the decay, the dope, the alcohol, the underworld of crime and racial hatreds which erupt ever more frequently throughout the continents. Ours is the most violent age since the world began.

There is the violence of the deprived and discontented, of guerrillas and nationalists, of black power and youth frustrated by the failures of the old. This is one more protest against paternalism, its caution, patronage, double-dealing, its selfish manipulation of the hopes and happiness of mankind, its gambling with the souls and bodies of men, its murder of idealism by the slow death of a thousand qualifications.

There is the violence of the establishment, of good and upright citizens who say their prayers and go to church, violence exercised by remote control, for these men would never soil their hands with blood. American Puritanism has been killed forever beneath the tons of high explosive used in Vietnam. Men of high principle, with a sense of the awful burdens of power and of America's mission to all mankind, men who long for the great society of brotherhood at home and an end of barbarism among the nations, have unleashed the fury of hell on helpless Asian villages.

But there is also the violence of the reactionaries, those who have no desire for liberty, equality, fraternity. Some of these, like the convinced believers in apartheid, justify their excesses in religious terms; some even sing "The Old Rugged Cross"; but at bottom there is hatred born of fear and the end is not anarchy but annihilation, as was seen in national socialism.

Not all protest is violent, as has been widely demonstrated in recent years. The great marches, not-

ably on Washington in 1963, though they have sometimes had the effect of taunting and provoking the reactionaries, have often been as peaceable as powerful.
The entry of Jesus into Jerusalem on the Sunday before his passion, assuming it took place as the traditions
assert, must have been far less impressive.

As in our historical sketch, we may appropriately
refer to the spirituality of protest. The worst violence
is the physical and secular counterpart of those uninhibited prayers of complaint and imprecation which
pour from the psalmists and the prophets. The marches
themselves are a kind of liturgy which must mean far
more to many who want to change the world than the
playacting of processions in church.

But one of the most interesting spiritual phenomena
has been the rise of the hippies. The word derives from
the jitterbug term "hep," which came into vogue during
the 1930's and meant to be "with it." This was changed
to hip during the bebop and beatnik era, and, having
fallen briefly into disuse, was revived to describe the
vast numbers of young people—tens of thousands—
probably more like hundreds—in the United States alone,
who, with the help of hallucinogenic drugs, enact a
nonviolent protest against the American, or Western,
way of life, with the slogan "Make Love, not War."
They have left their homes and work and colleges to
live a free community life in which the conventions of
society are disregarded. By the summer of 1967, there
were hippie enclaves in every large American city, from
Boston to Seattle and Detroit to New Orleans. Their
bodies, often scantily clad, are sometimes painted with
gay floral devices and slogans of love. They wear

blossoms, beads and bells and live to the strident music of beat groups. They are responsible for the word *psychedelic*, which pertains to a mental state of calm, intense, sensual perception induced by certain drugs.

The movement is a fascinating combination of back to nature and the wish to return to the land of childhood, the fairyland where all desires can be instantly gratified. Henry David Thoreau of *Walden* fame is one of their prophets, as is Aldous Huxley, whose book *The Doors of Perception* in which he describes the beatific vision he was vouchsafed after taking mescalin, could be called one of the foundation documents of hippiedom. Their saints include, of course, Gandhi, and a pantheon of Hillel, Christ and Buddha. The Beatles' practice of transcendental meditation is closely linked with the world-wide upsurge of some young people to challenge the materialism and jaded values of Western civilization by a search for ecstasy and peace.

In all these contrasted protests against the world of technology and empiricism there is spirituality of differing kinds. It lacks morality. In violent types, it deliberately flaunts all the conventions of compassion for its own ends. The hippies have an implicit code. *Time* magazine for July 7, 1967, to which I am greatly indebted, summarized it as follows:

Do your own thing, wherever you have to do it and whenever you want.

Drop out. Leave society as you have known it. Leave it utterly.

Blow the mind of every straight person you can reach. Turn them on, if not to drugs, then to beauty, love, honesty, fun.

These permissive ethics are valid for a protesting minority, but they would not be sufficient to organize human life through the world. Many young people, not all of them dropouts, would appear to feel that individual morality is less important than social justice. Not only may this end justify violent means, the guns of Bonnie and Clyde devoted to the cause, but some young intellectuals cannot see the correlation between personal transgression of accepted codes and the evils of the world. If it comes to that, the concept of sin is not found of much use either in diagnosing or curing the ills of the *psyche*, except as an atavism that needs to be got rid of before sanity can reign. Conventional morality may be blamed for the ills of mankind, since it has imprisoned the conscience of the rich and is but an elaborate system for justifying things as they are. There is a reluctance to think that the real troubles of the world have anything to do with the fact that a middle-class girl at college may sleep with several different men before she marries one of them (if indeed she does), especially since the availability of safe contraceptives may make it less likely that the result will be an unwanted child.

Yet more conspicuous than spirituality without morality is spirituality without theology. "No matter where we place our sound-detector, whether here or in Vietnam, in New York or in the Congo, in Berlin or in Cuba, we pick up the same notes everywhere: sighing and crying out, complaining and accusing, laughing and rejoicing in bewildering confusion. . . . For the situation out of which prayer springs remains, even when prayer itself ceases. It remains the situation of the world even when one brackets God out." [9] There is a spirituality of protest and of violence which would rend the heavens with a clenched fist and a mighty shout; but there is no God in heaven to be summoned from his throne. As an expletive it might be yelled "God has forsaken us," but never "My God, my God why?"

Similarly, for the nonviolent, the spiritual experiences they seek are not related to any specific belief about the universe. Meditation is a technique which relieves the tensions of life in our hideous world and may indeed transport a man to a transcendental realm of love from which he will return ennobled. But the realm is a state of mind, not communion with a God who is other. Any way to ecstasy is valid. Hashish may be as good as a guru.

Thus we uncover one of the paradoxes of our time, in which, as the Bishop of Durham has said, "We have a sort of spirituality which is devoid of God." [10] This means that we must now take a further look at the breakdown of theology.

[9] Gerhard Ebeling. "What Remains If God Is Eliminated?" *The Drew Gateway*, XXXVII, Nos. 1 and 2, pp. 24–25.

[10] Ian T. Ramsey, *Theology Today and Spirituality Today*," in *Spirituality for Today*, edited by Eric James, London, 1968, p. 82.

4 The Undermining of Christian Theology

We have already made plain that the intellectual and technological revolutions of our time are not congenial to orthodox Christian faith and devotional discipline, but perhaps the most remarkable fact is that professed Christians themselves are among the loudest critics of the tradition and of the life of the churches. Indeed, though scientific humanists and atheistic communists are usually hostile, the vast majority of people are benevolently indifferent rather than opposed to the churches, while many skeptics deplore Christians' questioning of positions they cannot themselves accept, and feel that the churches must stand or fall by their historic faith and forms. Perhaps there is something in Christianity itself which makes some of its adherents especially sensitive to the spirit of the age in which they live, as well as vehement against all false and idolatrous worship even of Christian *mores* and intellectual constructions.

The attacks—Christian and non-Christian alike—come from both the strength and the failures of modern man. He has come of age, not in a moral sense, but in the sheer fact of his mastery over his environment. It is as though he had been given the key of the house and can go in and out and undertake vast changes without reference to an almighty Father or supernatural land-lord, of whose existence his daily experience rarely makes him conscious. On the other hand, society is very sick. Yet the Christianity of the churches does not seem capable of effecting a cure. It has been the highly paid and privileged physician of the Western world too long and has nothing to offer save its outdated diagnosis and conventional nostrums. The fact that it claims to be a worker of miracles only strengthens the impression that it is a charlatan and must be dismissed.

But it is not the empirical or pragmatic test alone by which Christianity as it has been taught for two thousand years is tried and found wanting. Its theo-logical scheme no longer seems credible. Its conception of God, the position it accords to Jesus Christ, and its understanding of human nature are all assailed by the contemporary world view.

To each of these we must turn in a moment, but first we must notice that the Christian dissatisfaction with traditional theology is not altogether a cold intel-lectual disbelief or an impatience with the life of the churches and a disdain for the unimaginative conserv-atism of their ordinary members. It is an intensely sensi-tive response to the age of Auschwitz and its unspeak-able crimes for which there would seem to be no atonement. There is a high emotionalism about the "death-of-God" theologians and they may justly be said to deal in poetry rather than logic. Did not Altizer say to a reporter that his Christian vision of the death of God came upon him like an old-fashioned Methodist revival experience? Death-of-God liturgies have been

THE UNDERMINING OF CHRISTIAN THEOLOGY 99

devised—another instance of spirituality devoid of theology.

A common and very serious criticism of Hamilton and Altizer is that their teaching is a subjective and emotional reaction to the realities of the world without the control of the essential steadying rationalism of the Christian tradition. This is a movement within American Protestantism, which rejoices in its freedom from history. Catholics would have kept their heads better, for they have a longer memory and are more conscious that the sufferings of mankind and the cruelties of which we are capable are age-old and have been perennially reckoned with in Christian theology, even though technology makes them worse than ever. Yet the Church has too often stifled passion and the strange varied forms of enthusiasm for it to rest content with so smug a rejoinder, even if it be intellectually valid. The transcendental monstrosity of evil demands a transcendental response even if it be the exposure of "the 'dead God' of the century whom people worship." [1]

CRITICISMS OF THE IDEA OF GOD

We have seen that empirical philosophy does not demand a God. Man can manage without that hypothesis in the ordering of his life and the exploration of the universe and, although his organization of human society can hardly be regarded as a success, there is no

[1] Ulrich Simon, A *Theology of Auschwitz*, London, 1967, p. 102.

proof that in our age submission to a transcendent creator would make much improvement. Indeed it might be oppressive and inhibiting. Man must learn freedom and independence. He is the master of his own fate, the captain of his own soul, and he must realize this and walk erect and bravely on into the terrible yet glorious world of the future. If he is forever looking over his shoulder at big brother who is watching him, he will become twisted and tortured, he will be thinking about God and his own unworthy self rather than about the world and his neighbors. To many people today, the words in which the young Newman described the consequences of his evangelical conversion sound incredibly introverted and selfish. It made him rest, he said, in "the thought of two and only two absolute and luminously self-evident beings, myself and my Creator." [2] Similarly, John Wesley's *cri du coeur* in the previous century seems individualistic and otherworldly:

I have thought, I am a creature of a day, passing through life as an arrow through the air. I am a creature come from God and returning to God: just hovering over the great gulf; till a few moments hence I am no more seen; I drop into unchangeable externity! I want to know one thing—the way to heaven; how to land safe on that happy shore. [3]

When one reads John Bunyan's *Grace Abounding*—or, from another age and tradition, *The Spiritual Letters* of Dom John Chapman—one is tempted to wonder "Was it worth it?" Would not these men have been

[2] J. H. Newman, *Apologia pro Vita Sua*, Fontana, 1959, p. 98.
[3] John Wesley, Preface to *Standard Sermons*, Annotated E. H. Sugden, London, 1935, p. 31.

saved from dire agonies of soul and given liberty to serve their fellows even more notably if they could have been free of God, or at least of the idea of a God so intimately near and concerned that he would not let them alone while they swallowed their spittle? Perhaps their struggles were necessary in the evolution of human experience, but the question which should bring us to Gethsemane is not "How may I find a gracious God?" but "How may I find a gracious neighbor?"

There is also the irritating claim of Christians to a special knowledge of God. This is particularly evident in the pietistic prayers of evangelical groups and religious assemblies. They are often singularly blind to the signs of the times and cantankerous and quarrelsome among themselves but they address the supreme being with great intimacy as though he was much more present with them than amid the spiral nebulae or abroad in the struggles and triumphs, wonders and abasements, joys and sorrows of the world.

And if, in devotional practice, belief in God translates itself into monopolistic claims, academic theology, at least of the schools, is often worse and more nauseatingly presumptuous. It gives the impression of reducing God to a system. He becomes the unmoved mover, the static first cause, himself beyond suffering yet willing to answer prayer if it suits his purpose. Those who claim that God has answered their prayers, and produce not unimpressive evidence to prove it, heighten rather than diminish the problem and make God arbitrary and unjust, for why should their petitions be heard when others are seemingly ignored?

In a remarkable essay which deserves wider proven-ance than a commemorative volume seems to have given it, the late Kenneth Kirk, Bishop of Oxford and author of the renowned Bampton lectures on *The Vision of God*, wrestles with the problem of George Müller, founder of orphanages. He never asked for money, but *prayed* and, apparently, never failed to find in his post the amount he needed:

Here was a man of undoubted prayerfulness, and his prayers were answered day by day before all the world. But the answer came not necessarily because his prayers were more urgent, or more infused by faith, or more in conformity with God's immediate intentions, than many others; they came that God might show, in the instance of one remarkable life, how much He loves to receive our prayers, even though at times (and perhaps very often) His purposes do not permit of His "answering" them in the form in which they were uttered.[4]

The explanation is as devout as it is ingenious, but it is hardly satisfying to the man of the twentieth century. The thought indeed is in harmony with a long Chris-tian tradition and would probably have appealed to John Bunyan. Some principle of selection or election has been found inevitable if Christian theology is to try to reconcile the inequalities of life with the purposes of a just and loving God. Even so it does not establish either his love or his justice. If God's purposes allow him to make an example of George Müller in order to encourage people to pray, though they cannot neces-sarily expect any help for their orphanages, why do they

[4] "Prayer in War-Time," from *Beauty and Bands*, London, 1955, p. 53.

not allow it always? On what principles does God choose to answer some prayers and not others? Is he not guilty of teasing men into communion with him? It is better to be agnostic here than become involved in such theodicy; better to rely on what Robertson of Brighton called *"truths of feeling"* [5] than reduce the mystery of being to an explanation which, failing to satisfy the mind, betrays the heart.

The real difficulty is that it is impossible to reconcile the world as it is, even at its most healthy, with the unfolding purpose of omnipotent goodness. And any systematic theology which seeks to provide a clear and intelligible scheme of solution fails somehow to do justice to the grandeur and the horror of experience, to reduce to abstraction the splendor and the tragedy of life's ever-moving drama. This is where the Barthian protest against natural and philosophic theology should find echo even in the heart of an atheist.

The erudite theologian will, of course, be able to refute most objections and claim that the classical doctrine of God has been misrepresented and misunderstood, that if all its nuances were appreciated and its full structure studied, it would be seen to be as undisturbed by the criticisms of our time as the walls of some ancient castle by a peashooter. Finely orthodox stylists such as E. L. Mascall and Austin Farrer in England have shown this.

But I nearly wrote "as a giant in armor by a smooth

---

[5] F. W. Robertson's sermon on "Wrestling Jacob" was preached on June 10, 1849, and later printed as *Jacob's Wrestling, Sermons on Bible Subjects*, London, Everyman's Library, undated.

stone." David toppled Goliath and the point is not that traditional dogma is not massive enough to ward off every attack; it is that somehow, as Ian Ramsey says, it does not seem to mean anything in "the world of race-riots, redundancy, over-crowding, juke-boxes, guitars and drugs, motorways, supermarkets and civic communities." [6] Where the Christian concepts are able to be used at all, they seem as full of relevance as an attempt to quell a riot by a Latin decree, or else they demand so many qualifications that they become unintelligible.

DOUBTS AS TO THE NATURE OF MAN

The conduct of evolution, though it is not incompatible with belief in a Creator whose work is not finished but in whom all creatures fulfill their destiny, has cast doubts upon the uniqueness of man. He is an animal with some remarkable powers of being able to understand his environment, to control it and to communicate. But in the development of his upright stance and his large brain, he has lost certain faculties possessed by other creatures and he still belongs to the animal kingdom. If his distinction consists in him being a living soul, then there is no indisputable scientific evidence that this has any existence apart from his bodily organism. So much of the spirit or personality seems to depend on biochemistry, and bodily changes can transform the mind. Personality too is inseparably linked with environment. I am myself because I was

[6] Ian T. Ramsey, "Theology Today and Spirituality Today," in *Spirituality for Today*, London, 1968, p. 77.

born in twentieth-century England of a certain ancestry. If each individual is unlike any other, it seems a tremendous leap beyond the evidence to aver that each one is capable of such a relationship to God—if there be a God—that he still survives after the body dies.

Our age has seen a tremendous change in the attitude to death, and there is no truer indication of its belief about man. The vast increase in population may be partly responsible. More men are born into the world and more die. No longer are there so many village communities of a few hundred persons, for each one of whom the passing bell may toll and a sacred place with a marked grave be found in the churchyard. The older liturgies made of death and burial a great solemnity. There was no undue attempt to soften grief, to make mourning as painless as possible (and funerals an industry), to dispose of the body with the least trouble and then go on to the next. Death meant the judgment and life was a preparation for it. Every aid of Christian fellowship and counsel was sought. All the seventeenth- and eighteenth-century manuals of devotion include lengthy advice on this. Robert Nelson, an Anglican layman, wrote on the Christian festivals and this is one of his questions for Easter eve:

What ought then to be the great Concern of a serious Christian?

To fit and prepare himself for a holy and happy Death, in which he ought to use the greater Care and Caution, because a Mistake in this Matter is irrecoverable, and never to be retrieved. We can die but once and eternal Happiness or eternal Misery must be the Consequence of it. And happy is that Man whose Mind is so well fortified as to be able to meet the *King of Terrors*, not only without Fear, but with some Degree of Comfort and Satisfaction.[7]

The *Book of Common Prayer* has in its "Order for the Burial of the Dead," what Iris Murdoch, the English novelist, calls "words of such terrible weight":

Man that is born of a woman hath but a short time to live, and is full of misery. He cometh up, and is cut down, like a flower; he fleeth as it were a shadow, and never continueth in one stay.

In the midst of life we are in death: of whom may we seek for succour, but of thee, O Lord, who for our sins are justly displeased?

Yet, O Lord God most holy, O Lord most mighty, O holy and most merciful Saviour, deliver us not into the bitter pains of eternal death.

Thou knowest, Lord, the secrets of our hearts; shut not thy merciful ears to our prayer; but spare us, Lord most holy, O God most mighty, O holy and merciful Saviour, thou most worthy Judge eternal, suffer us not, at our last hour for any pains of death, to fall from thee.

They were softened and sentimentalized until the crucial matter at death was not the relationship to God but to the friends left behind. The emphasis was on the consolation of the mourners and the often insincere and false adulation of the deceased. This is less able to survive in the world of the secular city than the old, awesome solemnity. Perhaps indeed the doubts about the soul and its survival may purge us of sentimentality and make us grimly and soberly realistic about death, the irreversible coma into which some enter in a

---

[7] Robert Nelson, *A Companion for the Festivals and Fasts of the Church of England*, 32nd ed., London, 1815, p. 410.

moment, others after a weary lingering life in the shadows. Even the Christian can be but an agnostic here.

What does seem to be a fact of contemporary existence is that the imminence of death no longer makes men preternaturally serious. "Forefancy your deathbed," counseled the Puritan Samuel Rutherford, and Alexander Whyte, the great Edinburgh preacher who died in 1921, repeated his words often and told his hearers to make a reading list for their last illness. Most men today would regard that as morbid or, if they acted upon it, would as likely include P. G. Wodehouse as Holy Scripture or a book of devotion. Ronald Gregor Smith, in the introduction to *Secular Christianity*, chooses as his image of modern man Helmut James Graf von Moltke, a young German aristocrat and one of the martyrs Hitler made, who seems to have been as winsome as Bonhoeffer and politically wiser. We may be a little dubious as to whether Gregor Smith's choice is altogether representative. It somewhat weakens our confidence in his book from the start, for is a landed gentleman of the 1930s really typical of our culture now? Yet Moltke's attitude to death, though affirmative of Christian faith in the Lutheran tradition, is sanely twentieth-century. He writes to his wife after the sentence:

I do not in the least have the feeling that has sometimes overcome me, that I should like to see everything once more. But neither do I feel at all "otherworldly." You see that I am happy as I talk to you instead of turning to God. There is a hymn with the words, "for he who holds in life to thee is ready to die." That is exactly how I feel. . . . I do not concern myself with God or with my death.

He has the inexpressible grace to come to me and concern himself with me.[8]

There is God-talk there, of course, and soon those who die will not know any hymns, even to make them "this worldly" to the last. But it shows what could be a benefit of our agnosticism. Moltke does not try to be solemn, to prepare himself specifically for death or to think holy thoughts. He is quite natural. He does not plunge into elaborate exercises of prayer and self-examination or try to work himself up into a religious state. He turns to the human being he loves best.

Another good result of our uncertainty about human nature and destiny could be that we become more aware of the importance of this life. We dare not presume to be content that Lazarus should be left in his sores to beg, because we believe that in the world to come he will be more than compensated; we must allow him the dignity of a human being in this world, for he may have no other.

THE ENIGMA OF JESUS CHRIST

It is amazing that so many who feel that faith in God is meaningless still hold fast to Jesus, so that the old jibe against the Catholic modernist can be revised: "There is no God and Jesus Christ is his Son." William Hamilton is as passionate a devotee of Jesus as was Bernard of Clairvaux: "Jesus is the one to whom I repair, the one before whom I stand, the one whose

[8] R. Gregor Smith, *Secular Christianity*, London, 1966, pp. 16–17.

way with others is also to be my way because there is something there, in his words, his life, his way with others, his death, that I do not find elsewhere. I am drawn and I have given my allegiance." [9]

We could pile up quotations from other radical thinkers, which show a similar attitude. Perhaps here we have another instance of what we have noticed as one of the historic distinctions of Christian spirituality, that between theocentric and Christocentric devotion. These theologians are so dominated by Jesus that God is excluded altogether.

There is no doubt that they are all to some extent the children of Karl Barth and have been influenced by his Jesus positivism. Barth's strident claim that God is known only in Christ has become allied to the pressures of secular existence to give the conclusion that it is only Christ whom we can know. All the same, this devotion to Jesus is somewhat strange and illogical for three reasons.

First, although no one now seriously denies that Jesus was a historic figure, it is clear that we do not know sufficient about him to write his life, and that the records we have are all several decades later than the events they purport to describe. They are indeed the reminiscences of his life and teaching, preserved in various communities of the Christian dispersion and adapted to local needs. We know far less of the Jesus of history than we do of many of the figures of the ancient world and almost all men of consequence since. Years ago, Goldsworthy Lowes Dickinson, the Cambridge

[9] William Hamilton, "The Shape of a Radical Theology," *Christian Century*, LXXX, II, 40, p. 1221.

don whom his biographer and his bedder (and his English publisher, Sir Stanley Unwin) regarded as the best man who ever lived, said this:

My difficulty about Christianity is and always has been that Christians make the centre of their faith the historical existence of a certain man at a certain age; I daresay he *did* exist, though that has been doubted. But if he did, what was he really like? I cannot think religion can depend on such uncertainties.[10]

What is more, the story of Jesus is told in the categories of a far-off, prescientific age. To read the first chapter of St. Mark's gospel or the last chapter of St. Matthew is to be transported into an alien world of signs and portents, in which doves descend and angels from heaven, supernatural voices are heard, mental derangement is attributed to demon possession and earthquake to the direct intervention of God. It used to be fashionable to say that certain of the gospel sources "heighten the supernatural," and this is true, but no account can be made intelligible to modern man without an unscrambling of myths and a translation of concepts. A constant work of translation must go on and the man of the twentieth century with so much else to preoccupy him must wonder if the complex operation demanded is really necessary.

In so far as more is discovered about Jesus and the situation in which he lived, it will become more obvious that he did not think as we do and that it is not

[10] E. M. Forster, *Goldsworthy Lowes Dickinson*, quoted by A. R. Vidler, *Objections to Christian Belief*, London, 1963, p. 59.

easy to set him in our world, much less find in his teaching a program for society today. He was a Palestinian of the first century who seems to have been convinced of the imminence of the end, as the inauguration of the kingdom of God, in a way in which man today, in spite of the dire possibilities of our time, is not. It is not legitimate to attribute to him our notions of purpose or, for that matter, of the existential decision of faith. He thought neither as Harnack nor as Bultmann, neither as Harry Emerson Fosdick nor as Paul Tillich. Even in his personal dealings, in so far as we may trust the accounts, he sometimes seems fierce with his opponents and ruthless with his relatives and friends, and not the bourgeois ideal of graciousness and exemplary behavior (though this may make him more congenial to some today). Dennis Nineham, of Cambridge, in an important paper, has cautiously prophesied that in the next years "the figure of Jesus will be increasingly rounded out by the addition of a first-century dimension and that in the process the picture will not only be enlarged but considerably modified, and that in ways which will not make it more immediately acceptable to twentieth-century Europeans." [11]

Secondly, such knowledge of Jesus as we have, depends scandalously on the witness of the first Christians. Radicals such as William Hamilton and Paul van Buren might reply to the first criticism that precise historical details do not matter. A photograph of Jesus is

[11] Dennis Nineham, "Jesus in the Gospels," printed in Norman Pittenger (ed.), *Christ for Us Today*, papers from the Fiftieth Annual Conference of Modern Churchmen, held at Somerville College, Oxford, 24–28 July 1967, London, 1968, p. 57.

impossible, and if we try to paint a portrait we shall use the pigments of our own age and give him the features of our imagination. But a silhouette, however blurred, is enough, for this enables us to see that "humiliation, patience, and suffering are the ways God has dealt with man in the world, and thus are also the ways the Christian man is to deal with the world." [12] Alternatively, a silhouette gives us "the norm of the Christian perspective" which "is in the series of events to which the New Testament documents testify, centering in the life, death and resurrection of Jesus of Nazareth." [13]

This would be my own reaction to the lack of detailed historical certainty. But this leaves us, as we have said, with the Church, that long memory which straddles the centuries, imperfect, confused, blurred by the varied experiences of differing ages, and the conflicting philosophies of many civilizations, distorted by controversies and hatreds, yet apart from which there would seem to be no Christ at all. Faith in Jesus is tenable only if in some sense one says "I believe in the Church." But radical theologians show a hearty desire to abandon the Church tradition.

Thirdly, the New Testament shows us a Jesus who saw his own significance entirely in his relation to God. This is the unanimous testimony of the gospels and the letters. His mission was to lead men to the Father. The great commandment was "Love the Lord your

[12] William Hamilton, *The New Essence of Christianity*, New York, 1961, pp. 106–107.

[13] Paul van Buren, *The Secular Meaning of the Gospel*, London, 1963, p. 156.

God." This is what Jesus taught and it was for this that he died. One of the least disputed facts of his experience is his filial consciousness. But if God is dead, or gone dead in our world, if the whole notion is now a hindrance to Christian living, what is the value of Jesus, whose undoubted faith in God makes him either deluded or irrelevant in his main assertions? We can admit that in his eschatology Jesus may have been mistaken and still salvage a good deal; is there anything left if we deny completely his doctrine of God?

Paul van Buren does his best with John 14:9, 10: "He who has seen me has seen the Father; how can you say 'Show us the Father?' Do you not believe that I am in the Father and the Father in me?"

"Father" is the word which Jesus apparently used frequently in cases where his contemporaries might have used the word "God". It presents all the problems which arise when we try to analyse the word "God". The further explication of this word, however, is not the only, nor even the best, way to understand this passage, for the passage itself suggests a *via negativa* of an odd sort. The author asks us to stop "looking for the 'Father' ", for we shall not find him and the quest is beside the point in any case. Silence is the first and best answer to questions concerning the "Father." There are many "gods" and many "lords," but for those for whom the freedom of Jesus is contagious, who have been so touched and claimed by him that he has become the criterion of their understanding of themselves, other men, and the world, there is but one "Lord": Jesus of Nazareth. Since there is no "Father" to be found apart from him, and since his "Father" can only be found in him, the New Testament (and this passage especially) gives its answer to the question about

"God" by pointing to the man Jesus. Whatever men were looking for in looking for "God" is to be found by finding Jesus of Nazareth.[14]

It must be confessed that this is an outstanding instance of plain words being twisted to conform to presuppositions. It amounts to the distortion of embarrassing evidence. Radicals are worse than Catholics in reading their own preconceived ideas out of scripture; and in some cases, their basic accuracy is doubtful.

Thomas Altizer admits unequivocally the difficulties of basing a faith for today on the Jesus of history. He goes to the kenotic (self-emptying) Christology of Phillipians 2:5–11, and allies this with the prologue of the fourth gospel to find in the Word made flesh, the self-emptying, i.e., death of God. But this is no event in Palestine long ago, it is what is happening now in our world. If God is incarnate this means that he is irrevocably bound up with the historical process and if this leads men to admit that God is dead, then it is so, and "Christian theology must proclaim the death of God if it is to witness to the Word of faith." [15]

It is easy to write this off as poetic fancy. It has insufficient intellectual toughness to win many adherents. Yet it is as we have seen, the result of hypersensitive response to our world of secularism, which is the age of Auschwitz and it is more consistent than the Jesus-without-God of Hamilton and van Buren.

[14] Paul van Buren, *op. cit.*, pp. 146–147. There is a searching critique of this exegesis and of van Buren's whole position in a lecture by Peter R. Baelz of Jesus College, Cambridge, in *Faith, Fact and Fantasy*, London, 1964, p. 47 ff.

[15] Thomas J. J. Altizer, "Creative Negation in Theology," *Christian Century*, LXXXII, 27, p. 866.

WHITHER SPIRITUALITY?

Christian theology seems to lie in ruins, then, preserved and tended like some medieval castle by the
British National Trust, but of no use in the contemporary conflict except perhaps as an occasional tourist
attraction. And God is unreal and, possibly, a distraction from the achievement of true humanity in a better
world; man must reckon with the possibility that this
life is all and must be inspired and comforted, not dis-
tressed; Jesus, though somehow men cannot escape his
uncanny fascination, is an enigma. Faith in him is dis-
concertingly bound up with faith in the Christian community and can have no intellectually satisfying basis
apart from the idea of God, which is so meaningless
today.

What price spirituality? We seem to be left with a
combination of philanthropy, politics and mysticism.

Radical thinkers are not quite sure whether to welcome secularization or not. Some hail it as the victory
of Hebraic and Christian ideas over Greek and regard
it as the logical continuation of the process which
begins in scripture and, though he may not have known
it, was supremely advanced by Jesus Christ. Others feel
that its harshness and horrors need to be corrected, possibly by some of the techniques of Eastern religions.
But all realize that, like Carlyle's young lady and the
cosmos, we must accept it.

The parable of the sheep and the goats is the favorite
text of many radicals, not because of its weird mythology of the great assize, but because it tells of Christ
coming in the form of the hungry, the stranger, the sick

and the prisoner. True prayer is love of neighbor, not conversation with an imagined personal God, unseen and in heaven, but encounter with men who are all around us.

Philanthropy, however, is but an alleviation of men's condition, not a social change. So spirituality is politics too. Since the governments of the world all are parties to the *status quo*, politics means opposition, protest, sometimes violent, sometimes nonviolent. If the liturgy of the sacrament is the shared meal, and that of the word either personal greeting or group discussion, the great public act of worship is the march.

Yet our engagement to the world needs some inspiration and we ourselves must have, at times, some withdrawal from agitation and good works. Like the Primitive Methodist William Clowes, who could "sink into God" while the housework was going on, there are those who can be dissolved into ecstasy in the blare of pop music or amid the harsh dissonances of industrial life. Others need some ecstatic experience, induced in various ways, possibly by drugs; others are inspired by heady, spine-chilling, poetic notions, such as the death of God. Modern mysticism rests on no metaphysic or coherent explanation of the universe and it does not accept the creed of any religion as final. It selects, uncritically, from all faiths those techniques which seem of most help. In this it is as empirical as the age.

It would be agreed, however, that some guiding principles outside immediate subjective experience are required if the world is to be shaped in the ways of love and freedom. Simply to be involved without any clear idea of the purpose is sentimental nonsense and leads to chaos. If then spirituality is in part political practice, theology becomes political theory.

But the time has come to examine in greater detail how Christian thinkers and spiritual guides, other than those of the extreme death-of-God school, have reacted to our world.

PART III

Toward a Spirituality
for Today

5 Theological Reconstructions

Not all who accept the need for an agonizing reappraisal of the Christian tradition are so extreme as the death-of-God theologians, but very many thinkers are convinced that the primary concern of the Christian life must henceforth be with this world, with history, not a supposed beyond, except insofar as this is in the midst of the events of living. Some feel that the extremists are of great value in showing the utter futility of any attempt simply to rehabilitate the tradition. If there is a grave of God—or of a certain idea of him—we must not linger around it, either in lamentation or in attempts to call up the ghost, else we shall simply be dwellers among the tombs with no living faith. We must regard the grave as a milestone in the Christian march.

Such would be the view of Harvey Cox, who bids us look for the God who is to come. "If the present wake is for the God who *is* (and now *was*), this may clear the decks for the God who *will be*. . . . The doctrine of God would become theology's answer to the seemingly irrefutable fact that history can only be kept open by 'anchoring' that openness somewhere outside history itself, in this case not 'above' but *ahead*. . . . The only

121

future that theology has, one might say, is to become the theology of the future!" [1]

To arrive at this conception, Cox combines the ideas of two contrasted but, in his view, "seminal minds of our era," Pierre Teilhard de Chardin, the Jesuit whose works were not allowed to be published during his lifetime, and Ernst Bloch, a renegade Marxist. Teilhard has had such influence, in Great Britain at any rate, as to be almost the object of a cult. Some Roman Catholics believe that he has been more influential in the promotion of liberality than the second Vatican Council itself. His appeal lies in the fact that he is a visionary, who takes both science and theology with great seriousness and seeks to reconcile them in terms of cosmic purpose. The key passages for his thinking are St. Paul's descriptions of the travail of creation in Romans 8 and of the cosmic Christ in Colossians.

It is true to say that the majority, both of professional scientists and professional theologians, regard Teilhard somewhat dubiously and in the end his place in Christian history may well be that of devotional writer and liberator rather than philosopher. But Cox, who has been greatly influenced by Marxism which is also a visionary creed, sees him, together with the atheist Bloch whom he deems the more important thinker, as a prophet of hope. "The one examined the way cosmic space and geological time seem to dwarf man, the other how history seems to buffet him. But

[1] Harvey Cox, "The Death of God and the Future Theology," an essay which has appeared in various places and forms and is now reprinted in On NOT Leaving It to the Snake, London, 1968. The sentences quoted are pp. 11, 12 of that volume.

neither became discouraged; both saw hope in man's growing capacity to apply science and critical reflection to the shaping of his own destiny." [2] Where Teilhard is so congenial to the secularists is in his opinion that, before the world can be converted to the heavenly promises of the gospel, Christianity must be converted to the promises of earth.

Cox is also much impressed with the work of another Roman Catholic, Leslie Dewart's *The Future of Belief*. This had a fascinating origin in that it was commissioned by Herder and Herder, a Catholic firm, in an answer to a book they had courageously published by the French Communist Roger Garaudy. Dewart, while not disputing his Church's faithfulness to divine revelation in each succeeding age, feels that the time has come to translate the gospel into the terms of a dynamic modern philosophy and to break the shackles of a static Hellenism. This has caused controversy among the theologians of Dewart's own communion, and it has been criticized vigorously, not least on the grounds that it misunderstands the theism it disparages, and is weak in the history of thought. Cox approves of it because it seeks to free God both from the scholastic notion of being and the liberal idea of personality— the one too scholastic and imprisoning, the other too restrictive for modern man. God becomes the limitless possibilities and horizons of the future, though since these are *present* with us now in hope, so is he. This retains transcendence of a sort for these are truly "above all that we can ask or think," but it does not demand any concepts foreign to everyday experience and brings

[2] *Ibid.*, p. 9.

God out of the seminar and the sacristy, with their technical, in-group language, into the secular world. The initiative remains with us and herein lies the awful fact of our freedom. "History can actually fail." Hell may not be a punishment willed by the vengeance of God, but it is a real and eternal—in the sense of definite and irreversible—possibility for the future of mankind. It is the fact of Christ which bids us hope for heaven in history.

Harvey Cox apparently believes that, though God is not dead yet, not even in the carnage of our time, he would die if the future failed completely. Cox does not write much directly about the life of worship and prayer, but he has a passage on the mission of the Church in the world of cities, which sees it as symbolized in the names of three books of the Bible: Exodus, Psalms and Revelation.[3] Exodus means that the Church is a pilgrim people forever on the march from slavery to freedom, hankering after the security of Egyptian (or traditional) bondage, but always forced to go forward if it is to survive. And its proper company is not that of the pharaohs of the earth, the establishment, but of the disinherited and dispossessed, the hungry, the outcast, the victim of discrimination. Cox does not use the symbolism of the passover which dominates Exodus. He would not be happy with the concept of a once-for-all deliverance or with anything which encouraged too frequent a backward look, though the idea of the past being made of present power through memory would enrich his philosophy of history. Eucharistic worship, which the second Vatican

[3] *Ibid.*, pp. 110–11.

Council interprets in terms of the paschal mystery, does not seem to interest him. He is doubtless afraid of it because it may absorb into the sanctuary what should be let loose in the world. But it is a pity that he is not more specific about the place and forms of worship since his next title, Psalms, symbolizes the Church as the community of celebration. What distinguishes Christians from non-Christians is that they are aware of what God is doing. The gospel concerns all men. "Everyone has a part in God's drama. Men of faith have the added privilege of knowing the author, so that they can thank him for what he has done, not just for us, but for everyone." The traditional language is rather a shock and it would be interesting if Cox could develop these ideas more closely in relation to the book of Psalms with its complaints and protests as well as its praises. Finally, the Church, like John of Patmos, must be the company of those who see visions, who look beyond the present to the future even though they can but describe it fantastically. This could save us from becoming mere fodder for computers and stir us by divine discontent out of that complacency which is as much a peril for technocrats as for Christendom.

A different secular theology is that of Ronald Gregor Smith. His tantalizing and difficult, though intriguing and pregnant book, *Secular Christianity*, ends with an epilogue on prayer. If Harvey Cox is a Christian from the Baptist tradition who is convinced that Christianity must recognize its Hebraic kinship with Marxism as a philosophy (though not as the political organization of Stalin or Ulbricht), Gregor Smith is a Scottish Presbyterian and confessed disciple of Bultmann. If, for Cox, the great consequence of the fact of Christ is hope, the Church advancing gaily though humbly through the secular world to meet the God who is to come, for Gregor Smith it is faith, commitment in history to the eschatological reality of Christ. That last phrase which, though it is used in exposition, demands as much unscrambling as many of Gregor Smith's own sentences, means Jesus of Nazareth, who once lived and died, proclaimed as the one in whom God's final and redemptive act has been done in human history.

Gregor Smith uses history, defined with the most satisfying and subtle precision, to mean what happens to the individual now as a result of the encounter between his present and all of the past which is accessible to him. Thus, although Jesus is a figure of the past claimed to be the once-for-all act of God and the consummation of history, he becomes history for me and his end is realized in my life only as I am brought into relation with the recorded events of his ministry and death. So, "the end is not yet."

Compared with Cox, Gregor Smith is muted and subdued. He is just as antimetaphysical and as insistent on openness to future, but he has far less social optimism, hardly mentions a specific problem and writes much more in the classical evangelical terms of forgiveness. Cox marches to the strains of "We Shall Overcome"; at times, in Gregor Smith, there is the echo of a German chorale in a minor key.

No sign is given to faith, not even the empty tomb of the crucified. Could faith be attended by miracles, it would not be faith at all. The scandal of the Easter faith is "not that we are asked to accept as a verified

piece of 'history' an anti-historical dramatic intervention of God in the form of a miraculous sign . . ."
but "that we are invited to believe that here in the life
and death of a man God has entered into man's historical existence and in this life and this death has
acted out his own being, as a being for men and not
against them judging them in their self-contained pre-
tensions, and forgiving them, not giving them over to
the logical end of their existence, in meaninglessness,
futility, death and nothingness." [4]

It is Christian faith which is the source of secularism,
since it liberates man from the false other-worldliness
of religion and plants him secure in history. Modern
secularism is willfully ignorant of its roots, is at once
brashly optimistic and deeply despairing and leads to
drab subtopian monotony the world over if not, indeed,
to the dehumanizing and destruction of man, the
creation of a race of daleks. Gregor Smith is not as
lyrical about the culture of cities as Harvey Cox tends
to be. But the corrective to the superficial and bogus
secularism of our world is not a return to religion; it
is the true secularism of the man of faith, who lives
entirely in this world with Christ.

Faith is not observable or empirical. Gregor Smith
would not approve of the Puritan and Wesleyan tests
which the believer could apply to his life in order to gain
assurance. One would infer that, for him, Christianity
is not likely to make a notable difference to the social
order, though it must constantly be related to the problems of life in the world. The life of faith is hidden
with Christ in God and not so universally intelligible

[4] *Secular Christianity*, p. 103.

and attractive that men will hail Christians as their allies in human causes or be swept into the Church in droves. The hope of "one Church renewed for mission" would not impress him. It is too worldly and triumphalist, though he does not use those pejorative terms. His true Church would be a theological discussion group, "looking together at their own particular problem." This does not advertise and its discipline is not placarded among men. He is no sacramentalist, though the view of the past, which is Jesus being made accessible through the enacted memory in the Eucharist should appeal to him. The definition of the Church as the community in which the word is preached and the sacraments duly administered would be for him too restrictive, too pietistic, too apt to lead to preoccupation with trifles from validity to millinery. Yet he is moved—as who would not be—by Symanowski's description of a group of six young married couples meeting in East Germany to discuss the meaning for their own lives of the universal military training law. They made little progress until someone suggested they celebrated the Lord's supper, which was done by a layman with elements drawn from the kitchen of the house.[5] Like Cox, for Gregor Smith the Church is on a pilgrimage and is not given a map in advance; but one feels that, for him, the journey will be even harder and less exultant. He is as deeply aware as Bonhoeffer, of the inevitability of suffering and that much of the time secular Christianity will mean to watch with Christ in Gethsemane.

The epilogue on prayer needs more translation than

[5] See *The Christian Witness in an Industrial Society*, p. 84 ff.

most of the other chapters and I hope that the following paragraph gives a correct rendering. Gregor Smith deplores the idea of prayer as a help for happy living, and like George Macleod and John Robinson, finds the little books useless. "Prayer is to be understood as the anticipation in the whole of our existence of that one End which is the reality of God. . . . It is the engagement of the whole life in the hope of the End in Christ." This is a large and encompassing definition, very much in the terms of the Lord's Prayer itself of which the central petition is the eschatological "Thy kingdom come." Such prayer is only possible, as St. Paul knew, in the Holy Spirit. We, of ourselves, cannot pray as we ought, but the Spirit helps us, the Spirit through whom we cry Abba, Father, and stand in the same relation to God as did Jesus. Such prayer is not a spiritual activity, in the sense of being a holy withdrawal into elevating or ecstatic communion with God for our own comfort or improvement in abstraction from the world. It is indeed this very prayer in the Spirit which places us beside Christ in the garden, where he prayed his own prayer "Abba, Father" and, after the agony, "Thy will be done." This took him not to the easy success of the poised and integrated personality, but to the desolation of the cross. It did not summon legions of angels to his deliverance but left him in utter reliance on the power of the Spirit alone. "The Spirit is the only power in the world. But this Spirit is power in powerlessness. 'Only a suffering God can help.'"

In his latest book, *Exploration into God*, the Bishop of Woolwich questions whether he himself is rightly

numbered among the secularizers, though his great
theological concern is with this world. In *Honest to
God*, he wonders whether prayer "in the light of the
incarnation is not to be defined in terms of penetration
through the world to God rather than of withdrawal
from the world to God." [6] Prayer which so often spins
a cocoon around the devout protecting them from
reality, should in fact help us to bear reality. What is
more, many people cannot pray in a rarified atmosphere. Let them go apart from the world and they
find themselves in the arid wastes of introverted bore-
dom and barenness. And so he writes of "prayer in the
midst of life," of "seeing the diary in depth, preparing
on the telephone to meet our God." The test of worship is how far it makes us more sensitive to "the
beyond in our midst," to Christ in the hungry, the
naked, the homeless, the prisoner. Only if we are more
likely to recognize him there, after attending an act
of worship, is that worship Christian rather than a
piece of religiosity in Christian dress.

In the sacrament of Holy Communion, Christians
have the perfect representation of this, "the proclamation
to the Church and to the world that the presence of
Christ with his people is tied to a right receiving of
the common, to a right relationship with one's neighbour." But he recognizes that this rite can become the
most religious act of all, typifying withdrawal from the
world into a realm over against the secular.

In *Honest to God*, there was a certain tension be-

[6] *Honest to God*, p. 97. All the other quotations are taken
from the same chapter, "Worldly Holiness."

tween the idea of God as the ground of our being,
which has affinities with mystical theologies of the
interior life and, as we saw when we cited Vladimir
Rodzianko's critique, is not uncongenial to followers
of the apophatic or negative way, and the prophetic
and Biblical world affirmation of the teaching on prayer
and morality. In *Exploration into God*, the bishop
attempts ingeniously to reconcile the two, and points
to a new model theology of the incarnation in terms of
pan-en-theism—"the belief that the Being of God in-
cludes and penetrates the whole universe, so that every
part of it exists in him, but (as against pantheism)
that his being is more than and is not exhausted by
the universe." [7] He feels that this is the theology of
Teilhard de Chardin, for whom God fills the universe,
"shining forth from the depths of every event, every
element." And yet there is no absorption of the individual in the absolute. "Even in the intensest moment
of identification the distinctions of creature and Creator
remain." Pantheism, on the other hand, "makes for an
unhistorical quietism, without political cutting edge or
involvement with neighbour. And it plays down evil
and suffering as partial and illusory." John Robinson
was stimulated to this particular approach by a novel
of the Rumanian ex-Communist Petru Dumitriu, called
Incognito. The descriptions of the storyteller's reactions
to torture are not unlike those of the present Bishop
of Birmingham, then of Singapore, when he suffered at

[7] The definition from *The Oxford Dictionary of the Christian
Church*, ed. F. L. Cross, 1957, quoted by John A. T Robinson,
Exploration into God, pp. 83–84.

Japanese hands during the Second World War, and was able to see Christ in his cruel tormentors, as he tried to think of them as little children.

What is difficult is to bless the material world which contains the Central Committee and the *Securisti*; to love and pardon them. Even to bless them, for they are one of the faces of God, terrifying and sad.[8]

At last, in his filthy cell, the author comes to understand the divinity of Jesus Christ, "the one who had most deeply and intensely loved, and who had conceived the parable of the lost sheep: the first of a future mankind wherein a mutation of human hearts will in the end cause the Kingdom of God—the Kingdom, Tao, Agarrtha—to descend among men."[9] This insight, for the bishop, would be prayer.

In his closely packed chapter on the spiritual life, "The Journey Inwards," Robinson quotes Dag Hammarskjöld's dictum: "In our era, the road to holiness necessarily passes through the world of action." He would probably agree with the reversal of Peguy's aphorism, "Everything begins in mysticism and ends in politics," and say, rather, that it is as we are involved in the world of personal and social relationships and try to love it that we see the glory of God shining through and find ourselves standing with God at the creative center of the universe.

This is very different from both Harvey Cox and Gregor Smith, neither of whom is interested in mysti-

[8] Quoted from Robinson, *Incognito*, p. 90.
[9] Quoted, *Ibid.*, p. 91.

cism, being much more limited by the biblical and
Western tradition. Cox comes nearest when he draws
on Teilhard de Chardin and talks of vision. But this
for him is more secularist and political. He quotes
Karl Rahner: "Christianity is the religion of the absolute future," and the glory which we glimpse in our
dreams is a glory to be revealed one day in the life
of society on earth, which must inspire our action and
lead the churches "away from their nostalgic dream of
the rural past and into the peril and promise of the
urban future." [10] Prayer for him, in Dumitriu's cell
would certainly include a resolve to combat injustice
and to devote his sufferings to a future world in which
the captives were set free.

As for Gregor Smith my feeling is that he would
agree with Kierkegaard that mysticism has not the
patience to wait for God's revelation and feel that it
results in a sentimental romanticism rather than the
stark realism of faith, which asks for nothing but Christ.
In the prison cell, prayer, for him, would be the realization of his own powerlessness and his impotence to
do anything other than watch with Christ in Gethsemane. His only comfort would be in the knowledge
that the eschatological crisis of the cross would be
reconstituted in his own experience; but he would not
be solemnly and consciously trying to think about God,
he might recall his friendships or the best moments
of the past, "a chorus ending from Euripides," a Mo-
zart sonata, a baseball game or the torrent of Niagara.

[10] On Not Leaving It to the Snake, p. 140.

PROCESS THEOLOGY

Only John Robinson's anti-metaphysical stance would seem to debar him from joining the numerous company, who would see the way out from secularism and the death of God in a development from the philosophy of Alfred North Whitehead (1861—1947). The modern exponents of this include Charles Hartshorne, Schubert M. Ogden, John B. Cobb, Jr. and W. Norman Pittenger.

Whitehead was a mathematician and physicist, with a great interest in aesthetics. In some ways he may be compared with Teilhard de Chardin. Both began from a particular (though different) science, both sought to develop a comprehensive metaphysic which would unite all human experience, both found existing terms inadequate and had to coin new words as they went on. Whitehead has not the glamour of the Jesuit, for obvious reasons. His works were not denied publication by Church authority nor have his writings the mystique of Catholicism. But he is the greater metaphysician.

It has been said of Whitehead that "he shows us experience as arising out of a vast nexus of interrelationships." [11] Whitehead's metaphysics is constructed not from any given distinction between natural and supernatural, but from a close study of human experience, particularly perception and understanding. "The key notion . . . is that the energetic activity considered in physics is the emotional intensity entertained in life." [12]

[11] Dorothy M. Emmet, *The Nature of Metaphysical Thinking*, London, 1945, p. 234.
[12] A. N. Whitehead, *Modes of Thought*, Cambridge, 1931, p. 231, quoted by D. M. Emmet, *op. cit.*, pp. 228–29.

Whitehead's is a philosophy of organism and process. In his relatedness to the universal process, God himself is "in process" too. This means that he is limited. "It is not true that God is in all respects infinite. If He were, He would be evil as well as good." [13] Thus the old problem of God's supposed omnipotence and the existence of evil does not arise and there is no need to take refuge in paradox which is so easy an escape from uncomfortable decisions. ("A theological paradox, it appears, is what a contradiction becomes when it is about God rather than something else.") [14] We must simply recognize that the static perfection of God is derived from the old notion of substance, which should be replaced by process. Instead of the scholastic *being* there should be *becoming*. God is perfect, not because he is unchangeable, but because he is the living and indeed growing God. In our experience that which does not grow is not a perfect being but a dying or dead one. God's unchangeableness consists in the fact that he is *always* alive and *always* growing. "That he is ever changing is itself the product or effect of no change whatever, but is in the strictest sense change-less, the immutable ground of change as such, both his own and all others." [15]

If, with Pittenger and others, we find the clue to the process in love and say "God is love," then perfect love,

[13] A. N. Whitehead, *Religion in the Making*, Cambridge, 1926, p. 138.

[14] Charles Hartshorne, *The Divine Relativity*, Yale University Press, 1948, p. 1.

[15] Schubert M. Ogden, *The Reality of God*, London, 1967, p. 60.

though it cannot deny itself and is eternally constant, is yet dynamic and active in events.

It is important to do justice to Whitehead by remembering that for him there are two aspects of God's nature, inseparable in reality, but to be distinguished in thought. There is the aspect which is in relation to the world and affected by it—the "consequent"—and the aspect which is unaffected, absolute, unchanging "primordial."

All this depends on Whitehead's doctrine of prehensions. Think of the monkey's prehensile tail and it will be seen that to prehend means to grasp or cling, though in Whitehead, also with an idea of feeling after. As we thus grasp at experience or cling to it, energy is transmitted and a new unity results, which Whitehead calls a concrescence. An entity which is growing is a concrescence of prehensions. But we must select from the manifold impressions and experiences which come to us and we do this by our (mental) sense of importance. This is what helps us to organize the confusing multiplicity of matters of fact.

Now Whitehead insists that God is not the exception to all metaphysical principles but their chief exemplification. He prehends too. At the same time, God gives the initial aim to the process and supplies the lure, the attraction of all things to its fulfilment.

It is not surprising that years ago Father Lionel Thornton, of the Community of the Resurrection, sought to interpret the incarnation in terms of Whitehead's philosophy. This resulted in a most difficult book, which has been criticized as not doing full justice to our Lord's humanity, and need not concern us here except as an instance of the way in which some thinkers feel that in Whitehead there are great resources for the re-statement of Christian faith.[16] A recent simpler and more satisfying attempt to use Whitehead to help our understanding of Christ is made in an essay by P. N. Hamilton of Trinity Hall Cambridge, *Some Proposals for a Modern Christology*.[17]

It is easy to make deductions for the life of prayer. Prayer is a form of prehension—our openness to experience and to the God who is in it. It is a vaster activity than the direct and conscious approach to God through time set aside to address him. Yet it is directed towards God and the fulfillment of his aim in the process of evolution, and the initiative is his. "No one comes to me except the Father draw him." Work may be prayer and so may listening to music or perceiving the mysteries of nature, yet only insofar as these lure us into identifying ourselves with the "love that moves the sun and all the stars." And since prayer is our co-operation with the God who is in the process as well as its initiator, it may be said to affect him. It does not change his will, but our witholding of it in this wide sense of response and cooperation may militate against the cosmic process. As Whitehead wrote, "The immediate facts of present action pass into permanent significance for the Universe."

This is very similar to Teilhard de Chardin, whose "divine milieu" is, in effect, the process. "If we want

[16] Lionel S. Thornton, *The Incarnate Lord*, London, 1928. Criticisms include that of D. M. Baillie, *God Was in Christ*, London, 1948, p. 91 ff.
[17] Printed in *Christ for us Today*, edited by W. Norman Pittenger, p. 154 ff.

the divine milieu to grow all around us, then we must jealously guard and nourish all the forces of union, of desire, and of prayer that grace offers us. By the mere fact that our transparency will increase, the divine light, that never ceases to press upon us will irrupt the more powerfully." [18] Teilhard de Chardin uses prayer in the conventional sense. It is a deep desire, implanted by God, which is turned into request for the fundamental gift of illumination.

Teilhard is not treated by philosophers as more than a visionary, while Whitehead is clearly vulnerable to the criticism that he has constructed a kind of mythology and projected the terms used for the description of human experience into the whole of reality. The modern linguistic philosophers and the positivist theologians such as Karl Barth have made us forever doubt whether a perennial philosophy is possible and at the very least convinced us that the most satisfying metaphysical scheme will one day be superceded. Yet we should not yield to panic amid the rain of their fiery darts. Human experience is not necessarily an erroneous pointer toward ultimate reality and what coheres with it, in its broadest aspects, cannot be wholly at variance with the nature of the universe. Even if we would agree that theological and metaphysical statements are not about things in themselves, we may accept the valuable Tillichian distinction made by the Bishop of Woolwich and say with him: "But neither are they simply affirmations of my outlook or perspective on life. They are statements about the reality in which my life is

[18] Teilhard de Chardin, *Le Milieu Divin*, London, 1960, p. 125.

grounded as I respond to that reality at the level of 'ultimate concern' (as opposed to proximate concern—the level at which scientific statements etc. are true)." [19] This minimum allows us to agree with Schubert Ogden that process theology "enables us so to conceive the reality of God that we may respect all that is legitimate in modern secularity, while also fully respecting the distinctive claim of Christian faith itself." [20]

THE TRADITION REVISED AND REVIVED

Some theologians, particularly English Anglicans and European Catholics, would feel that the secularists are simply astute thinkers who work from a certain deposit of vestigial Christianity but who have an appalling ignorance of history. They are not sensitive to the men or situations of the past, and, while it is amateur historicism always to be looking for and finding parallels to contemporary problems, it is barbarian to assert that our world is so different that it needs a wisdom hitherto denied. Few theologians of note are so conservative as to feel that the tradition may be taken for granted. Our minds must be open and we may need to begin a lengthy and thoroughgoing exploration of the evidence without assuming any axioms.

> We shall not cease from exploration
> And the end of all our exploring
> Will be to arrive where we started
> And know the place for the first time. . . .[21]

19 John A. T. Robinson and David L. Edwards, eds., *The Honest to God Debate*, London, 1963, p. 252 ff.
20 Ogden, *op. cit.*, p. 56–57.
21 T. S. Eliot, *Little Gidding*, London, 1941.

An exponent of this method is David Jenkins of Oxford. He warned his Bampton Lectures audience in 1966 that:

If men had accepted what their generation found thinkable we should have had no science and precious little humanness. Nor do I see why we should succumb to the arrogant complacency of assuming that what we may call "the modern world view" is a final and decisive arbiter of what we, as men and human beings can or ought to think.[22]

As much as that of Bishop Robinson is his concern with persons. It is with this given that, for Jenkins, theology starts. But for him the possibility of personal life is guaranteed only through the Christian God, whose unquenchable love enters completely into suffering, though without threat to his unchangeable and imperishable divinity. "If God is dead man is dying," [23] and "there is no substitute for God":

I am increasingly convinced, philosophically and practically, that either this is true or everything is nonsense. In the end language won't hold together, psychology won't hold together, humanity won't hold together if you have to describe everything in terms of something else which requires something else to describe it in terms of.[24]

Prayer has two foci. One is persons responding to this transcendent personalness who is the God and Father of Jesus Christ. The other is grace which is the

[22] David Jenkins, *The Glory of Man*, London, 1967, p. 15.
[23] *Ibid.*, p. 65.
[24] From a so-far unpublished paper, "To Whom Is Prayer Addressed?"

awareness of the presence of someone other who gives resources beyond one's own. Jenkins is convinced that the ultimate basis for prayer must be Trinitarian.

That is to say, that you are concerned with the God who is wholly God and therefore wholly other, who is wholly incarnate in Jesus Christ, without in any way diminishing or detracting from the utter otherness of God, and who is also present in personalities and through personalities as the Holy Spirit.

He would commend all this to modern secular man by what he calls "focused awareness" and "openness to inspiration." The former is very like what in classical Christian spirituality has been called contemplation but it comes not at the end of a long process of discipline but at the beginning. It demands quiet attention to the whole of experience and dedication to a common worthwhile end. Openness to inspiration implies that prayer is of form of action rather than a form of thought in that it requires effort. This is particularly true in relation to the reading of the Bible. People's minds will be closed to its true inspiration if on the one hand they regard it as sacrosanct, or on the other as a tissue of tattered legends. If they treat it as a normal book to be studied honestly and dispassionately, they may well find that it captures their imagination so that they become possessed by its message, and responsive to the transcendent God with whom it deals.

Another careful theological study of the problems of prayer is found in John Burnaby's essay in the symposium *Soundings*. He reflects the bewilderment of modern man with the petitionary nature of so much

Christian prayer as evidenced in the earliest stratum of the New Testament and in so many of the liturgies. Yet to conceive of the will of God, in John Oman's parody as "the force of omnipotence directed in a straight line by omniscience" is contrary to the facts of this frustrated world. Does prayer make a difference? Burnaby suggests that the only answer is to restate the implications of the Christian faith. The kingdom of God is to be promoted in human history by no other power than the power of love and the power of God's love takes effect in no other way than through the wills and actions of men in whom that love has come to dwell. "To pray is to open the heart to the entry of love—to ask God in." And "The life that is released in the soul that has consented to the wooing of God's grace is no longer a life *of* the soul but the life and power of its union with God. And by that union the universal working of the love of God has increased." [25]

One of the great benefits of Burnaby's discussion is that it helps to transcend Heiler's famous distinction between mystical and prophetic types of prayer. The former is the prayer which seeks for union with the infinite and is largely contemplative, the latter is the prayer of faith and is largely asking. Heiler's dichotomy has been criticized by Burnaby himself in his *Amor Dei* long ago, but it is of great service in interpreting the history of Christian prayer. But the two types should really be different facets of one whole. As Burnaby says, contemplation and petition should not be regarded as two different ways of prayer, since the great petition is for union with the will of God, the

[25] John Burnaby, *Op. cit.*, p. 233.

practice of the presence of God, which nevertheless must always be active. "Thy will be *done*."

It will be seen that both Jenkins and Burnaby are in no doubt at all that the transcendence of God in some form is necessary to Christian prayer as is the doctrine of grace. Prayer is the opening of our hearts and lives to the power of love revealed in Jesus, which left to ourselves we neither know nor deserve.

Ian Ramsey, Bishop of Durham, has always been very sensitive to the charges of the logical positivists that religious language is meaningless and that metaphysics is impossible. He has therefore devoted much patient investigation to the symbols used by religion. These arise because of what Ramsey calls "cosmic disclosures." These he defines as situations which have come alive both subjectively and objectively. A normal flat piece of sense experience which may be described in mechanical terms, takes on a new dimension. A pop singer is an ordinary enough concatenation of physiological components. The noise he makes can be measured in sound waves, the energy he exerts in foot pounds. As a private individual there may be nothing unusual in his psychology or relationships. Yet through his art there is a tremendous, quasi-religious emotional effect, which is of profound significance to all who are involved in it. The situation becomes charged and the fans, who may be very normal teen-agers, are taken out of themselves. They are as gods in their transcendence of the conventions and calculations of commonplace existence. This is a cosmic disclosure. Insofar as something other than themselves confronts them (and other than the singer as an ordinary young man using his bodily mechanisms), they may be said to be recipients of a divine revelation. Perhaps a Whiteheadian category of importance is needed to distinguish between this, which may be a crude rather primitive disclosure, and a higher one. In any case it would be but one, possibly rather trivial, element in the consideration of a whole number of disclosures, some of which, like a prophet's call, might lead to a cultural revolution but all of which are the proper subject matter of theology. Each would probably have some focal point which Ramsey calls a model, which would come to stand for the disclosure itself. In a more religious age, God might be thought of as the great singer. Nearly always the model will be personal, not because the concept of personality comprehends the whole mystery of the universe, but because it is in personal relationships of some kind that disclosure situations characteristically occur.

In his lecture to the Parish and People Conference on Spirituality at Durham in 1967, Ian Ramsey developed the consequences of this for the life of prayer. Asceticism—a more intellectual activity than has sometimes been thought, a logical discipline and training of the mind—would be a preparation for disclosure and the ability to understand and assimilate it. "The traditional distinction between the purgative, the illuminative and the unitive would not be successive stages in the spiritual life (so much) as expressions of different inroads into an understanding of that life." [26]

To pray to God as a Person, our Father and our

[26] Ian T. Ramsey, "Theology Today and Spirituality Today," *Spirituality for Today*, p. 83 ff.

Friend, is legitimate provided we remember that this is "model discourse and it is only when we understand it aright that we shall see the function of words in prayer, and the end of prayer being that mystery, which all experience of God and his grace must inevitably in the last resort be." [27] The end of prayer is indeed silence, but a silence very like that of the early Quakers, "into which various models enter and from which various discourse originates." Ramsey quotes John Ciardi, who regards a poem as "one part against another across a silence." The silence is like a rest in music; it is "a point of balance between areas of discourse," the point at which a cosmic disclosure is most likely to happen.

Theology, on this understanding of it, will have a much more tentative character than formerly. Indeed much Western theology has killed the spiritual life because it has not done more than pay lip service to the divine mystery. It has claimed the key of knowledge, the map of the whole universe, the explanation of everything from the Eucharist to the end of the world. Henceforth theology itself must be more spiritual, an aid to prayer. But the cosmic disclosures arise out of life. They are not given in pious withdrawal, but in this world of race riots, motorways and juke boxes.

Elsewhere, Ramsey warns against looking for verifiable deductions. He contrasts Elijah on Mount Carmel with Jeremiah. Elijah's is a type of the prayer of faith, staking all on the fact that God will answer by fire and prove himself. Elijah is justified. But what God did for him in that vivid demonstration would bring its own problems and need to be interpreted with

[27] *Ibid.*

great caution in his future activity. Had God not so displayed himself, Elijah's religion might have been, in the long run, enriched. For Jeremiah, on the other hand, ". . . it was in failing to find anything resembling, let alone able to be misunderstood as resembling, verifiable deductions that Jeremiah's religion rose to new and distinctive heights." [28]

Ramsey's use of the Mount Carmel story is quoted by Peter Baelz, Dean of Jesus College, Cambridge, in his important study of *Prayer and Providence*. Baelz is not uncritical of Ramsey here, because he is not sure that faith will forever be enriched if there is no evidence at all that God hears our prayers and is aware of our needs.

Baelz's book is an attempt to relate the vigorous anthropomorphism of scripture to an acceptable philosophy which takes due account of the world as we know it in the twentieth century. It is a reasoned reinterpretation of the Christian tradition, which, while it ignores no difficulty, is as acutely critical of the critics as of Christianity itself. It nowhere disregards or despises religious experience, and it does not, like so many discussions, both traditionalist and secular, loftily assume that the prayer of asking, prayer which is conversation, is philosophically intolerable and religiously naïve. It is a quiet but incisive counterattack on many unchallenged assumptions of our secular age.

Baelz affirms the transcendence of God and yet retains the personal analogy, or, as Ramsey would say, model. But he goes farther than Ramsey and is clearly

[28] Ian T. Ramsey, *Religion and Science: Conflict and Synthesis*, London, 1964, p. 71.

seeking some kind of unitary and cosmic interpretation, such as makes Teilhard de Chardin so attractive to so many, Baelz included. "The ascription of personality to God is a determined attempt to hold together the religious and moral sides of human life in a unity, since it is in interpersonal relations that we discern the possibility of a harmony of giving and receiving, of acceptance and activity." [29]

Belief in a personal God, providentially active in the world is a way of seeing the world as a whole, empirical facts and that which transcends them, the reality of good and of evil too, history, nature, individual existence and cosmic fulfillment. Prayer teaches us how to participate in the mind and action of God:

Because it flows from a recognition of what God has already done in and through Jesus Christ, prayer will always have the note of thanksgiving. Because it looks forward to what God has still to do in and through those who respond to his love, it will also have the note of petition and intercession. It has often been remarked that petitionary prayer is to be found at the centre of Christian communion with God. The reason for this should be clear if we keep in mind, first, the tension between the 'already' and the 'not yet', and, second, the co-operation which God seeks from man in the pursuit of his purposes. Petitionary prayer can then be seen for what it is, namely, the confluence of divine providence with human faith. Activity and passivity combine. Prayer is both a resting in God and a wrestling with God. In its essential character communion with God is not a participation of the senses in the processes of nature. Nor is it a submission of the mind to a rational necessity which determines all that happens. Man protests in the name of his moral and per-

[29] Baelz, *Prayer and Providence*, London, 1968, p. 88.

sonal freedom against such would-be divinities. Christian faith however, claims that communion with God and self-surrender to his will is to be found on the other side of moral protests, for it discovers that dependence upon God and participation in the divine life is a dependence on a Love which gives man his freedom and does not destroy it. Man's own being is penetrated by the being of God, yet without diminishment. The indwelling of God is the condition of his self-fulfillment.[30]

Baelz faces the difficulties of belief in answers to prayer in the sense of our being able to persuade God to do what otherwise he would not. His tentative conclusion is not unlike Burnaby's: "We may give the divine Love a *point d'appui*, so that through our prayer it may realise the possibilities which only in this way it can actualize." [31] Yet there should be no limit to our expectation and our faith.

Baelz's final paragraph is reminiscent of the sentences which end John Burnaby's Hulsean lectures on St. Augustine, *Amor Dei:* "Love never forces, and therefore there can be no certainty that it will overcome. But there may and there must be unconquerable hope." [32] Before that he is compelled to admit the suffering of God. This is no imperfection, though it is a limitation. It is rather the consequence of the fact that God is ever receptive and is temporal, not as we are, for whom time means change and decay, but in the sense that while his love is perfect, his joy increases and is enriched by the response of his creatures.

[30] *Ibid.*, pp. 100–101.
[31] *Ibid.*, p. 118.
[32] John Burnaby, *op. cit.*, London, 1938, p. 318.

Baelz refers to Whitehead but once and then a trifle disparagingly. Earlier he appears to tilt at process theology because, to quote the late George Woods, "We cannot rest in absolute change." Yet is his final view radically different from it bearing in mind Whitehead's "two-aspect" view of God and Ogden's suggestion that change is not unrelated to perfection and to constancy?

What Baelz would deplore is reductionism and in this he would find support in the Roman Catholic theologian Hans Urs von Balthasar. Romans, of course, have a more luxurious spiritual tradition than Protestants, which means that there are more layers of comfort to cushion them against the hard spikes of skepticism. They can peel off the gaudy covering of exotic and distracting accretions and still not suffer all the proddings of the secularists. The second Vatican Council was the culmination of a revival of biblical theology. The Roman Church now uses with ever-increasing fidelity the great concepts and images of the Bible and derives them for its faithful, not from liturgy alone, but from the text of the Bible itself. Yet its exegesis is often patristic and typological and seems to impose certain theological patterns upon the scriptures, rather than to derive its theology from them. The fine Mariological section of the Vatican Constitution on the Church, *Lumen Gentium*, uses the biblical interpretations of Irenaeus rather than of historical criticism.

Balthasar, however, has an essay on "Closeness to God," in which the rich historical approach to the Old Testament and the life of Jesus is seen to great advantage since Jesus is related to the religious background and archetypes which resulted from what Ian Ramsey would call "cosmic disclosures" of Israel's experience. Balthasar attacks the tendency to debunk which is current in so much of the contemporary approach to problems.[33]

" 'This or that is nothing . . .': life and spirit are nothing but a complicated structure of matter; moral good is nothing but what is most useful or agreeable to the individual or society; aestheticism is nothing but a branch of sociology; so-called evil is nothing but the expression of a biological condition." The nadir is reached with "true religion is nothing but ethics" or "love of God is nothing but love of neighbour."

Balthasar is most concerned with the question whether an immediate relationship with God is either possible or necessary in our time. May it not be an intellectually untenable distraction from true Christianity? He shows, on the contrary, that the whole ethical system of the Old Testament is based on covenant with God and that Jesus, who "understood and presented himself as the fulfillment of the Old Testament and even its embodiment," cannot be taken seriously apart from his consciousness of God. He called God by the unprecedently childlike and intimate name of *Abba* and constantly returned to the solitude, silence and depth of prayer from whence he drew his power.[34]

[33] Hans Urs Von Balthasar, "Closeness to God," *Concilium*, Vol. 9, No. 3, pp. 20–27, from which all citations are taken.
[34] It is interesting that J. Neville Ward (in *The Use of Praying*, London, 1967, p. 11) takes the view that we do not know enough from the scanty records to be sure of this latter point.

Thus he was enabled to be, as Barth says, "man *for* all men," not simply man *with* all men, and the gospels show him withdrawn as well as involved. He does his work, not only by dialogue but by confrontation. The inexorable love of the Father, of which he is the revelation, not only attracts but pursues, not only reconciles but judges.

Balthasar, who has already referred both to Barth and Kierkegaard, proceeds to develop this in terms both Protestant and Catholic. Before any awareness of modern thought or sensitiveness to what modern man will accept, there must be open, unprejudiced, hearing of the word of God.

This basic biblical demand was interpreted in the Christian Middle Ages in the sense that all Christian action must flow from a preceding act of contemplation. Later, Ignatius of Loyola interpreted it in a more biblical sense: at the origin of any specific Christian task lies an act of absolute openness rooted in the immediate nearness of God, an act of total readiness for all things, whatever God may put into his Word.

This comes very close to Luther's pure faith. It always reflects what Jesus required of his disciples: to put themselves in principle beyond any inter-human relationship. . . . This "listening", "contemplation" or "openness" of pure acceptance is without any doubt the basis of all prayer, which is only truly prayer when it rests on the unconditional acceptance of God's will (or at least tries to rest on this acceptance).

The demand of God may be present in a human "Thou," but not to full measure. Kierkegaard's "endless qualitative distance" between us and God must never be forgotten. It is the presupposition of our closeness to him, which necessitates a kind of death. "Hence all those who are sent by God come from some desert." At present there is too much "prayerless talk" in Christianity. Service of mankind, love of brotherhood and the neighbor is possible only after withdrawal to the wilderness where is the mount of God.

Balthasar's essay is fascinating for its reaction against secular Christianity and its suggestion that when we think we are most serving the present age we may simply be infatuated by the craze to debunk, the end of which is nihilism; for if you see through everything the result is nothingness. It shows that classic Catholicism and Protestantism probably have more in common than either of them has with religionless Christianity and it seeks to rehabilitate the classic disciplines of both traditions—contemplation and hearing the word. Prayer is not philanthropy, communion with God is not the service of my fellows and our awareness of the divine does not come primarily from human associations. This, Balthasar would claim, is the biblical doctrine and the truth to which the Christ of the gospels points. It is the essential presupposition of true Christian humanism and effective mission to the world.

Karl Rahner, the Jesuit, also writes in very Protestant almost Lutheran terms about the prayer of petition.[35] He acknowledges that intellectual sophistication and abstract, spiritless thinking have reduced prayer to a tranquilizer or, at best, an act of hope for success beyond this life. The prayer of petition is a problem. Can we by our "bawling and weeping move the heart

[35] Karl Rahner, "The Apostolate of Prayer," 1953, *Theological Investigations*, Vol. 3, p. 209 ff.

of God to intervene in this world?" It is our faith in
the incarnation, the certainty that God is forever committed to this world and human concerns which should
convince us that the prayer of asking is not in fact the
lowest but the highest form of prayer. "Why else is
the Lord's prayer not a hymn but a sevenfold petition?"
Similarly, Archbishop Anthony Bloom of the Russian
Orthodox Church has challenged the common opinion
that petition is a stage for beginners which the mature
have outgrown. "The ability to say prayers of petition
is a test of the reality of our faith." [36]

Karl Rahner's essay "The Apostolate of Prayer" is
such a call to prayer as would delight an evangelical.
He has one philosophic paragraph, "a kind of transcendental deduction of the truth of prayer." "Can there
be a phenomenon which rests in principle (and not
just in individual cases) on an illusion, while at the
same time it is real and efficacious?" But he goes on
to plead for more intercession. If we really pray for
the needs of men in our world then our piety is no
longer enclosed and introverted. Prayer creates love of
neighbor and helps us "to acquire some understanding
of the heart of the Lord." "Would it not be good if
there were many more such Christians to continue the
apostolate of intercession, who at every hour of the
eternal Good Friday of this world . . . hear to some
degree the rousing call 'Oremus'. . . ?"

If Rahner wants prophetic prayer, there has been in
our time a tremendous increase in Pentecostalism, a
return to enthusiasm, a waiting upon the immediate
inspiration of the Spirit. Behind it is a desire to claim

[36] Anthony Bloom, *Living Prayer*, London, 1966, p. 82.

the fullness of the gospel promises, as the name of a kindred organization, "The Full Gospel Business Men's Fellowship," indicates. Speaking with tongues is not only a phenomenon of corybantic movements outside the orthodox communions, it has invaded the traditional churches and the campus at Yale. It has even been manifest in the by-no-means "low" Church chapel of an Anglican bishop on the south bank of the Thames. It has not been so marked a feature of Christian experience since the New Testament and the Montanists.[37]

In an essay on "Religion and Enthusiasm," Professor H. D. Lewis of London insists that there can be no true religion without wonder, devotion and passion, travestied and "cultivated as spiritual luxuries divorced from spiritual reality" as they so often are.[38] "Religious truth that does not disturb us can never be genuine. . . . No vulgarity appalls like religious vulgarity. But we must not oppose it by a veto on all that is not amenable to direct rational discipline." As the antidote to the aridity of barren forms and undue cerebration, Lewis would recover the beauty and lyrical passion of Welsh hymnody.

PRACTICAL RESPONSES

But we have already strayed from theory to practice. Before we bring this chapter to a close, we must notice

[37] The subject is reviewed in Morton T. Kelsey, *Tongue Speaking*, New York, 1964.

[38] Printed in F. G. Healey, ed., *Prospect for Theology*, Essays in honour of H. H. Farmer, London, 1967, p. 35 ff.

briefly four published evidences of spirituality for our time and one almost unanimous conviction.

Prayers of Life by Michel Quoist is the product of a Roman Catholic group which met in l'Havre in the early 1950s. They use traditional techniques of meditation, but begin from wherever a man happens to be —on the subway, at the stadium, spending money, watching young lovers, glancing at a bookstall, reading the newspaper. Their theology is orthodox, they are verbal meditations, some of them very long, but they are daring, simply because they are so realistic and relate the truths of the gospel to concrete situations, setting it free of the sanctuary.

Quoist has had tremendous vogue and seems to have revived prayer for thousands, jaded by antique exercises and stifled by the stuffy atmosphere of a room whose windows are shut against life. It is ironic that there are many who in one breath assert that the idea of prayer as talking to someone is absurd, and in the next testify to the power of Quoist, or the more extreme chattiness of Malcolm Boyd's *Are You Running With Me, Jesus?* The deduction seems to be that the problem for the great majority is not theological or philosophic, but the remoteness of religion from the world with its long Good Friday and its secular Easter, and of that hell and heaven which are other people. Speech is their natural mode of expression, the sign of their humanity, but they want to use words which convey their real feelings not an artificial jargon, recondite and assumed, which deafens them to life.

Robert Raines's *Creative Brooding* provides Kierkegaardian reflections to awaken and provoke thought.

It is intended to provide some escape from the noises of civilization, not least of perpetual entertainment and what Russell Baker has called "the invisible orchestra" which "is spreading across the country like chestnut blight." Raines begins each of thirty-four readings with a passage from literature or journalism, a passage which conveys an experience from life. This connects with some text of scripture or religious verse and leads to a brief Quoist-like prayer of resolve. Once again, prayer springs from reflections on life, not from any contrived religious mood. A by-product of the method is that the Bible is seen as the book of life, human life, worldly life, but the chief purpose is to engage the mind preparatory to stabbing the heart. The variety of tones, in contrast to Quoist's lengthy variations in the same key, should make it even easier for the brooder's mind to become engaged, so that at the end he is compelled to make the concluding prayer or resolution. It is so much more valuable than to start with scripture, which at first seems so remote, so conventional.

Dag Hammarskjöld, Secretary General of the United Nations, kept a spiritual diary, which was published after his death. It was given the title *Markings* and, although a best seller, was found rather bewildering until Dr. Henry P. van Dusen attempted a correlation with the outward events of the great civil servant's career.[39] It is now possible to see the work as a remarkable twentieth-century lay example of the old Puritan advice to keep a diary. *Markings* shows that each outward event in Hammarskjöld's life was anticipated by

[39] Henry P. Van Dusen, *Dag Hammarskjöld: A Biographical Interpretation of Markings*, London, 1967.

an inward conflict, each battle was fought and won within himself before ever he was engaged in public affairs. It shows too that, after many struggles with skepticism, he was helped to return to the beliefs of his upbringing through the ethics of Albert Schweitzer, who also provided him with a modern key to the world of the gospels.

But the explanation of how man should live a life of active social service in full harmony with himself as a member of the community of the spirit, I found in the writings of those great medieval mystics for whom "self-surrender" had been the way to self realization, and who in "single-ness of mind" and "inwardness" had found strength to say yes to every demand which the needs of their neigh-bours made them face, and to say yes also to every fate life had in store for them when they followed the call of duty, as they understood it.[40]

As he progressed, he became more biblical, more sensitive to the Christian year and more conscious of the living God of Pascal and Buber.

Hammarskjöld is in some ways reminiscent of Thomas R. Kelly, who died in 1941, but whose *A Testament of Devotion* is likely to prove congenial to many seekers of our time. The Bishop of Woolwich is attracted by it and, since Kelly was a philosopher and much influenced by A. N. Whitehead, the process theologians will doubtless give the little book further prominence. Kelly was a Quaker and a dedicated seeker for truth. Just as Hammarskjöld, shortly before he be-

---

[40] From *Old Creeds in a New World*, a radio statement by Hammarskjöld at the outset of his secretaryship, reprinted in Van Dusen, *op. cit.*, p. 46 ff.

came Secretary General underwent a transforming experience in which he "answered *Yes* to Someone or Something," so Kelly in the late fall of 1937 achieved or was given a marvelous integration of his life. This resulted in certain lectures and papers, written in a limpid and effortless style, commending the interior life in the beloved community. Paradoxes were resolved in the deep knowledge of God within. "He plucks the world out of our hearts, loosening the chains of attachment. And He hurls the world into our hearts, where we and He together carry it in infinitely tender love." [41] Some of the old symbols of sacramental Christianity came alive for him, as they had for George Fox[42] and he spoke of feeding on the body and blood of Christ.

In a paper on "The Reality of the Spiritual World," Kelly concludes with a reference to the "bondedness" experienced in the "ceremony of the sacrament of Communion." "There is a way of continuing this communion through daily life. No outward bread and wine need be present, but inwardly we feed with our fellows from the Holy Grail, and meet one another in spirit." There is a surprising unanimity among contemporary theologians and all those who have engaged in the quest of a new and relevant spirituality that the great central act of corporate Christian worship, the Eucharist, has a power which does not change. We mentioned earlier the Lord's supper, celebrated, with what some would regard as dangerous informality, by the young couples wrestling with the conscription law in East Germany. An English theological student who a few

[41] Thomas R. Kelly, *op. cit.*, London, 1941, p. 43.
[42] See above, p. 65.

years ago wrote that linguistic philosophy had made any idea of prayer almost nonsensical, nevertheless found that the Eucharist, the local accepting community gathered around the representation of the self-giving Christ, could become what Paul van Buren, whose views are similar, would call "a discernment situation." Gabriel Fackre, who would mediate between tradition and radicalism believes that the way to greet the new age with joy and yet not to be captive to it is through Eucharistic theology.[43]

The one clear conclusion is simply this: ours is an age of empiricism and no philosophic forms or practices will be accepted unless they are seen to work. No declaration about God or the world or prayer will be heeded unless it coheres with what men actually know of life as they live it. No symbol or tradition of the past will be honored unless it reverberates again in our experience now.

[43] See *New Theology No. 4*, New York, 1967, p. 178 ff.

6 The Way to God

Much of the foregoing has been the summary and exposition of other people's views, a descriptive account
of the rich and varied tradition of Christian spirituality
and of the reactions to its apparent collapse in our
secular world. Some believe that we should accept the
disintegration as the logical consequence of Christianity itself and devise a spirituality of this world in
which love of God will be love of neighbor and prayer
active participation in the relief and conquest of the
many ills which threaten human life. Others, while not
disputing this, feel that some technique of meditation
and withdrawal is needed if we are to be socially effective and they would include some who would admit
the necessity of worship, of awe, reverence, amazement
and mystery, even if the content be that God is dead.
Others again think that, reappraised and properly understood, there is life in the old beliefs, forms and disciplines of historic Christianity and that the practice of
prayer through Jesus Christ our Lord with the help of
scripture and classic devotional guides may be com-
mended in our time. Yet most, apart from the very
conservative Catholics and evangelicals, would find it
difficult to believe in a supernatural realm over against
the natural or in a God who answers prayers by inter-

ference in the course of nature and history other than through his effect on the person praying.

What follows is a personal statement, which is not concerned with the interpretation of other thinkers, but seeks to outline the philosophy and practice of a spirituality for today.

Spirituality must begin from human experience. This does not simply mean "Pray as you can and not as you can't," though that is useful advice, provided it does not encourage too speedy a renunciation of effort. It means that the attempt to enter into a living relationship with the reality behind the universe must start from an interpretation of those disclosures made to me personally and to mankind throughout the ages insofar as they are accessible to me now.

This at once enlarges the scope of spirituality. It is not confined to religion as a specific department of human life like chemistry or sport. True, an old woman at prayer is a far more wonderful creation than the most superb computer ever devised, but hers is not the only way to God, to contact with the ultimate. The rapport between parent and child, intermittent and perhaps diminishing with the years as it may be, or between any two human beings who are friends though not necessarily in love, is the evidence of a beyond which is greater than their separate or united selves. The love that makes a man give up his ease or his all for a cause is more than egoism or enlightened self-interest and is of another dimension from the morality of honest trade or gainful employment. In art and music, humanity seeks to express desires and emotions, which are beyond the power of ordinary language and would push through the limits of the finite world.

The first task of spirituality will be to reflect upon experience and to revere those signs, even in the most ordinary relationships and situations, of that which transcends the merely mundane. John Betjeman's poem "In a Bath Tea-shop" is an example:

> Let us not speak, for the love we bear one another—
>   Let us hold hands and look!
> She, such a very ordinary little woman;
>   He, such a thumping crook;
> But both for a moment, little lower than the angels
>   In the tea-shop's ingle-nook.[1]

Many a pop song shows a similar awareness amid its harsh dissonances and trite words.

It is very important to remember that the experience which is the raw material of spirituality is not wholly pleasant and elevating. We must not select the good things of life and ignore the rest. A disclosure may come as well through the darkness at noonday as through the blaze of transfiguring light. A faith which does not make room for horror, injustice and pain is an escape from reality, not an encounter with it. This is why there is so much spirituality in the protest of our time, why we must reckon with prophetic prayer as well as mystic serenity; why a true religion will not simply accept the world but seek to change it, why the greatest revelation of all could be in the words, so graven on contemporary Christian hearts: "My God, my God, why hast thou forsaken me?" The man of prayer, like

[1] John Betjeman, *Collected Poems*, London, 1958.

Dantë or Bunyan, though he may not be capable of their artistic expression, will know what it means to descend into hell and his cry will often be out of the depths.

So much of our reflection upon experience will be on the past. This is not to say that prayer is the study of history or that spirituality is antiquarianism. It simply notes the fact that the moment of insight or disclosure has gone before we realize it and it only becomes objectified in our experience when it is no longer immediate. And yet reflection on it, which is only possible when it is past, brings it back again into the present.

Ritual and religious worship are corporate occasions of recall. Through symbol and ceremony they seek to recover and make contemporary past disclosures. Some rituals have been doing this, virtually unchanged, for many centuries, notably the Christian Eucharist. But this would not have a living power unless the events which it celebrates and sets forth did not seem still to find echo in the life of men today. "The Mother, the Child, and the bare manger: the lowly man, homeless and self-forgetful, with his message of peace, love and sympathy: the suffering, the agony, the tender words as life ebbed, the final despair: and the whole with the authority of supreme victory." [2]

Memory selects from the past and never reproduces exactly what happened. In any case this would be impossible when what is recalled and recollected is no mere earthly event but a discernment situation. It is

[2] A. N. Whitehead, *Adventures of Ideas*, Cambridge, 1942, p. 214.

remarkable that the writers of the New Testament are on the whole so prosaic and sober and that there is not more in the style of John, the Seer of Patmos. This shows that the narratives were inspired by authentic human experience of natural events even though each author and community expresses them differently, often in the clear terms of legend, and uses categories impossible for us. There is no chance of recovering the Jesus of history in the sense of knowing precisely what he was like, or being present as if in the body at each recorded event in his life. But we have even richer possibilities. Martin Kähler, sometime professor of theology at Halle, spoke of "the historic Christ in his fulfillment," the one on whom Christians have reflected throughout the ages, always with imperfect understanding and partial insight, sometimes heretically and superstitiously even when they were trying to be most orthodox, but who stands before us in so many different forms as the Man for God, who prevailed by love alone and won victory from defeat and offers us a way of redemption which breaks the bondage of causality.

Spirituality need not fear the most radical New Testament criticism. Indeed the less we feel we surely know about the Jesus of history, the more we are dependent on the Christ of faith and the one who, as we recall him, is fulfilled in our lives now. In some ways criticism is irrelevant to spirituality. We read the gospels and relate each passage to our situation without forever asking "are these the actual words of Jesus? Did this happen as the evangelist says?"

At the same time we must be honest. We must not

pick and choose those sayings and stories which most
approximate to our idea of Jesus and discard the rest.
"I cannot believe that Jesus said that" is the declaration
of a man who would make Christ in his own image.
About a great deal in the gospels, hard sayings and
tender, we can assert no more than "This is what some
of the early Christians believed Jesus said and did," or
better, "This is the impact which Jesus made on his
first followers as they thought about what they had
heard of him, in the light of their own experience."
The question for spirituality is the same as that which
Professor Leonard Hodgson posed for scholarship:
"What must truth be and have been, if it appeared like
that to men who thought and wrote as they did?" [3]

No spirituality is possible if there is utter contempt
for the past, for this does not simply cut the umbilical
cord, which must be done and which is often undertaken with far too much hesitation and reluctance; it
severs the arteries of our being.

No spirituality is possible without discipline. Too
often this has been harsh and unimaginative, an attempt to force men to lift themselves to heaven by
their own bootlaces. Some of the radicalism of our time
is born of the old conflict which Christians have traditionally described in terms of faith and works. It has
been some of those most committed to the disciplines
of daily office, regular sacramental confession and frequent communion who have rebelled against the burdensome irrelevancy of it all in a world at once so
enthralling and so desperate as this. Discipline for
discipline's sake is meaningless and vain. Neither can

[3] L. Hodgson, *For Faith and Freedom*, Oxford, 1956, I, p. 87.

a man by taking thought induce in himself the lure of the eternal. Discipline is our necessary response to those concerns which are inescapable. The poet says "I do but sing because I must," and this inner compulsion binds him to the desperate disciplines of prosody. The philosopher is driven to the quest to find the truth about the multiplicities of existence and, for this, he must, if necessary, give up all that he has. It is the pure in heart who shall see God. And purity does not mean freedom from sexual temptation; it means single-ness of mind in pursuit of some compelling and ulti-mate concern (which, incidentally, is the only way to deliverance from the lust of the flesh). For this a man will "scorn delights and live laborious days"; and to him, as to Thomas Kelly dedicated to philosophy, or to Dag Hammarskjöld committed to the service of mankind, the disclosure will be made. Though he may not use conventional words to describe it, he will see God.

It is probable that, for many people in our time, disciplines will need to be revised. Ten minutes a day, or regular offices, or even Sunday worship each week, may not be practicable as technology increasingly orders all. There is no valid objection to the alternative of a long weekend every three months for spiritual restoration, This, however, presupposes small com-munities, which will maintain an almost constant vigil of prayer and meditation, into which those more preoccupied with the world may from time to time withdraw. This is where the revival of Christian com-munities, monastic and otherwise, is so valuable, so essential. They will be seen not as honors schools of

holiness, but as companies fulfilling a particular voca-
tion for the good of all.

And yet it may be questioned whether this may not
perpetuate a dangerous misunderstanding of spirituality, a readiness to rest far short of the ideal, which is,
as Quakers and true mystics have so well understood, a
living of the whole of life in the presence of God.
At any moment the divine light may break in upon us
and we may practice an art of contemplation which
makes the words of Thomas Traherne no fancy: "The
dust and stones of the street were as precious as gold.
. . . Boys and girls tumbling in the street and playing
were as moving jewels." [4] This light will not blind us
to the darkness; apart from it, we should not be aware
of the shadows in which the world exists. Nor will it
make us less vehement in our protest and our politics.
Sometimes we must withdraw from the world completely and go apart into a desert place. Yet even there
we shall not escape distracting temptations and, like
Jesus and his disciples, we may need to abandon our
rest and quiet to answer the demands of men. The result was a greater miracle of God's presence than if
Jesus and his followers had been seeking it in solitude.
What we must disown is any suggestion that the disclosure of God is to be looked for only in the times devoted to deliberate contemplation, our retreats. Neither
is the discipline we need a matter of time set apart for
religious exercises. It is the direction of the whole of
our life. This is where George Macleod and John Robinson after him are so right in relating prayer to the
diary of each day. This is old spiritual wisdom. Baron

[4] Thomas Traherne, *Centuries of Meditations*, Oxford, III, 3.

von Hügel describes the counsel of Fénelon to the Duc de Chevreuse, who was much distracted in prayer. Let him begin each day by quietly running through in his mind what he would have to do and reduce each activity as much as possible, pruning it of all unnecessary detail and development.[5]

In an aphorism which has become notorious on the lips of those who can hardly have read it in context, A. N. Whitehead wrote that "Religion is what the individual does with his own solitariness." [6] He goes on ". . . if you are never solitary, you are never religious. Collective enthusiasms, revivals, institutions, churches, rituals, bibles, codes of behaviour, are the trappings of religion, its passing forms." It is impossible to dispute this and every recipient of profound religious disclosure would agree. True religion must be inward before it can be outward. But Whitehead does not conclude that religion is a flight of the alone to the alone, or decry the importance either of social action as a religious response, or of "the beloved community" of those who share a common knowledge of God and seek to encourage one another. Indeed, Whitehead's philosophy is of organism and interrelationships, of the value of the diverse individuals of the world for one another and of the merging of individual claims with those of the objective universe. He also says "Religion is world loyalty." [7]

The value of the group in spirituality has been re-

[5] F. von Hügel, *Essays and Addresses*, second series, p. 227.
[6] A. N. Whitehead, *Religion in the Making*, p. 6, also pp. 37, 48.
[7] *Ibid*, p. 49.

discovered in our time. The group is not always a company of the living. Dag Hammarskjöld was a recluse, religiously, who did not in his adult life seek the fellowship or sacraments of the visible Church, yet one of his "markings" for 1952 is this: ". . . through me there flashes this vision of a magnetic field in the soul, created in a timeless present by unknown multitudes living in holy obedience, whose words and actions are a timeless prayer. . . . 'The Communion of Saints'— and—within it—an eternal life." [8]

Similarly, Thomas Kelly, in his lecture on "The Blessed Community," writes of reading the scriptures "with no thought of pious exercise but in order to find more friends for the soul," and he goes on to recommend those devotional writings from the Christian centuries, which "speak the language of the souls who live at the Centre." [9]

But, clearly, one's faith and practice will best be sustained and fostered by regular meetings with a few friends, not necessarily kindred spirits, but ardent in their quest for reality. Such groups might be constituted as follows:

(i) They should be interdenominational and where possible multiracial, and should include non-Christians willing to share the same quest, with an absence of aggressive defensiveness on all sides.

(ii) They should not number more than twelve people, and should have a regular, though not too frequent, change of membership, so that while continuity is preserved and people get to know each other inti-

[8] *Markings,* London, 1964, p. 84.
[9] *A Testament of Devotion,* p. 71.

mately, there is no danger of the groups becoming cliques or cells of traditionalism.

(iii) Apart from the common mind of the group there should be advice and guidance from the resources of the Christian tradition. Sometimes this will be in the person of an individual minister or layman; but he will be a director not a dictator and will have an ad hoc rather than permanent position. Often guidance will come as the group puts its concerns and problems in a wider context or as its membership changes.

(iv) They may well use the customary methods of common and private Bible study, simple worship (perhaps the saying of an office) and, where possible, the Eucharist.

(v) Talk and prayer must issue in service and perhaps in political action, though the groups will represent no one party or political philosophy.

(vi) The Christian household may find renewal from this ecumenical pattern when it is based on the neighborhood. The devotions attending a family meal such as John Robinson has described could be an appropriate revival of family worship.[10]

We come finally to the heart of our subject. What conception of God should be the basis of a spirituality for our time? Here I speak most personally and without attempting to acknowledge all the sources of my own belief though many of them will be apparent from what has gone before.

[10] Cf. John A. T. Robinson, *The New Reformation?*, pp. 84–85.

God is that reality in which all things hold together, in which alone the diversity and confusion of experience is unified. Every existence exists in him. The personal pronoun, though inadequate and far from exhaustive, is not misguided. Personality is the highest form of being we know and God cannot be less than this, while to borrow Ian Ramsey's nomenclature, the personal "model" is the one which most appropriately describes the disclosures in which we are most aware of "the beyond in our midst."

The ever-present danger is to limit God by our categories. He may be limited by his own nature but that is different. We must be sure that our faith in God is adequate both for the realities of the world, in its strange confusion of glory and wretchedness, and to the mystery of God himself. A personal address to God has sometimes been nauseating, because it claims that he is so much at the disposal of those who use it, an assumption which all the objective evidence denies. The Book of Job may deserve Peter Baelz's strictures that it is not altogether free of the "headmaster" approach to religion,[11] but it ends with Job's hand upon his mouth in the realization that God is concerned with more than demonstrating Job's righteousness.

But God may be addressed when he cannot be expressed, and although the Bible contains much anthropomorphism, its doctrine of a God who enters into living, personal relationships, who is dynamic and not simply the unmoved mover, is truer to our knowledge of the world than the more classic idea of the serene

[11] *Prayer and Providence*, p. 56.

omnipotence who overrules all nature and history and whose triumph is certain once he chooses, in his own inscrutable wisdom, to exercise his sway.

Our theological formulations must be tentative, for we are not privy to all the counsels of God. Christianity has never begun from philosophy or tied itself to a metaphysical scheme. It has begun from lives and from the facts of existence. This is the meaning of that remarkable parchment, which the seventeenth-century Catholic and mathematician Blaise Pascal wrote and sewed into the lining of his doublet in November 1654, after a period of the most intense and agonizing prayer.

FIRE

God of Abraham, Isaac and Jacob; not of the philosophers and scientists.
Certainty, certainty. Feeling. Joy. Peace.
God of Jesus Christ.
Deum meum et Deum vestrum.
Thy God shall be my God.
Forgetfulness of the world and of all, except God.
He is to be found only by the ways taught in the Gospel.
Greatness of the human soul.
O righteous Father the world hath not known Thee, but I have known Thee.
Joy, joy, joy, tears of joy.
I separated myself from Him.
Dereliquerunt me fontem aquae vivae.
My God, wilt Thou forsake me?
May I never be separated from Him eternally.
This is life eternal that they might know Thee, the only true God, and Jesus Christ Whom Thou hast sent.
Jesus Christ
Jesus Christ

I separated myself from Him. I fled Him, renounced
                    Him, crucified Him.
May I never be separated from Him.
He is to be kept only by the ways taught in the Gospel.
                    Renunciation, entire and sweet.

Pascal is adamant that the only real God is the God
and Father of our Lord Jesus Christ. The place accorded to Jesus Christ in our doctrine of God is due to
two things:

(1) The Christ event provides the clue to the working of God in history and the Universe.

(2) Jesus himself is the supreme exemplar of faith
in the living God, the crown of the long Old Testament
tradition and one who had a unique awareness of God.

As we have said, there is much about Jesus that we
cannot know. From what we do know, it is clear that
he was not infallible and may well have been mistaken about many things. He was a Jew of the first
century, alien to our civilization and yet with a
haunting and universal appeal. His significance depends
on the faith in God for which he laid down his life,
and on the belief that, in his activity, we see the moving
pattern of the love which is the meaning of the whole
process of the worlds. God is so much involved in the
universe that he is mostly hidden by it, but every now
and then there is, as it were, an eruption ("disclosure"
if you want to retain the term we have favored most)
and, supremely, in Jesus and the cross.[12]

---

[12] I have borrowed this analogy from James A. Pike, *A Time
for Christian Candour*, p. 102. He defines a volcanic eruption as
follows: "If a given spot becomes thin enough, soft enough,
weak enough, that which underneath functions uniformly nevertheless manifests itself in a particular event."

There is a dialectic between the idea of God, which seems, philosophically, most true to the world of our experience and the biblical faith, which reaches its consummation in Jesus. The one answers the other and illumines it and the two together may give us the synthesis for our time.

We cannot retain the notion of divine impassibility, that God does not suffer. "Only a suffering God can help," and much of Christian prayer will be a suffering with him, the Gethsemane, which rehearses the cross and makes our warfare in the world, not painless, but easier insofar as the battle has been fought first in our own hearts. The spiritual life has intoxicating joys, but sore agonies too, not because it imposes artificial burdens and false fears, but because it is concerned with reality in which there is so much of evil. In chapter five, we quoted Whitehead's saying that if God were in all respects infinite, he would be evil as well as good. This is why the traditional doctrines both of impassibility and omnipotence are no longer tolerable. As an alternative, we may continue Whitehead's argument:

God is complete in the sense that his vision determines every possibility of value. . . . Thus God is the one systematic complete fact, which is the antecedent ground conditioning every creative act.

The depths of his existence lie beyond the vulgarities of praise or of power. He gives to suffering its swift insight into values which can issue from it. He is the ideal companion who transmutes what has been lost into a living fact within his own nature. He is the mirror which discloses to every creature its own greatness. . . .

God has in his nature the knowledge of evil, of pain, and of degradation, but it is there as overcome with what is good. Every fact is what it is, a fact of pleasure, or joy, of pain, or of suffering. In its union with God that fact is not a total loss, but on its finer side is an element to be woven immortally into the rhythm of mortal things. Its very evil becomes a stepping stone in the all embracing-ideals of God. . . . He transcends the temporal world, because he is an actual fact in the nature of things. He is not there as derivative from the world; he is in the actual fact from which the other formative elements cannot be torn apart.

But equally it stands in his nature that he is the realization of the ideal conceptual harmony by reason of which there is an actual process in the total universe—an evolving world which is actual because there is order.[13]

Prayer is the companionship of God. We must abolish class distinctions and Cassian's old snobbery of higher and lower levels. Enough that sometimes prayer will be with words and sometimes without, sometimes an intellectual activity, sometimes a simple regard. Purgation, illumination, union may not be three successive stages, but simultaneous, though often the order may need to be reversed and it is the union which leads to purity and light. To petition God may mark a very advanced point of spiritual progress which, in a world like this, requires great faith. The answer may never be by any immediate change of circumstances or redeployment of natural forces. Prayer does not bring rain or make wars to cease. God does *not* "send the snow in winter, the warmth to swell the grain," neither can he directly intervene to save the world from famine or from interracial holocaust. Yet, within the process, he is ever-active and ever-seeking those who will cooperate

[13] *Op. cit.*, pp. 138–41.

in his purposes of love. Answers to prayer are like the replies of a dear and trusted friend in conversation or by letter. They are assurances of love and illuminations of wisdom. They do not cause the heavens to fall or arrest the stars in their courses, though to us, they may indeed open heaven and make us lords of creation and send us out with joy to act and suffer for the truth.

We must not tempt God, or ask for signs, though sometimes, to the discerning, signs may be given. Our greatest inspiration will be through the fellowship of dedicated spirits and through the ancient rites and symbols of Christ, which fasten us as nails to the cross in which is all our hope.

And perhaps, in the moment of our greatest despair, when all seems lost, and we think that God is dead, some Hammarskjöld is somewhere saying "Yes" to God, or some other human being is committing himself to the irresistible way of holy obedience along the royal road of universal love.